**180 Devotions
and Worship
Activities for
Preschoolers**

HUGS FROM JESUS

Devotional

SALLY PIERSON DILLON

REVIEW AND HERALD® PUBLISHING ASSOCIATION
HAGERSTOWN, MD 21740

This book was
Edited by Jeannette R. Johnson
Copyedited by Delma Miller and James Cavil
Designed by Patricia S. Wegh
Cover designed by Tina Ivany
Illustrations by Mary Bausman
Electronic makeup by Shirley M. Bolivar
Typeset: 11/13 New Century Schoolbook

PRINTED IN U.S.A.

05 04 03 02 01   5 4 3 2 1

R&H Cataloging Service
Dillon, J. Sally Pierson, 1959-
    Hugs from Jesus.

    1. Children—Religious life.   2. Devotional
literature—Juvenile.   3. Devotional calendars—
Seventh-day Adventist.   I. Title.

            242.62

ISBN 0-8280-1567-8

BOOKS BY SALLY PIERSON DILLON

The Code Breaker
Little Hearts for Jesus
Victory of the Warrior King
War of the Invisibles

To order, call **1-800-765-6955.**
Visit our Web site at **www.reviewandherald.com**
for information on other Review and Herald products.

My Little Devotional

_____

Dedication

To Vanessa Barahona Hickerson, my honorary grandbaby:
You are growing into a wonderful little girl.
Have lots of fun as you learn to enjoy Jesus as your best friend.

To Saylin Rose Jetter:
Welcome to the world! Life here isn't always easy,
but Jesus has promised to be your friend and to never
leave you alone.

And to Charissa's little one:
Even though none of us have met you yet,
Jesus knows you and loves you and has a special plan
for your life.

Contents

Contents

Contents

Contents

Contents

Contents

Contents

Contents

Contents

Contents

Contents

Contents

Contents

Dear Mom and Dad...

Childhood is full of teachable moments. That's why, after God gave the Commandments to His people, He told them to "Impress them on your children. Talk about them when you sit at home and when you walk along the road, when you lie down and when you get up" (Deut. 6:7, NIV).

Along these lines, you'll find devotions in this book that are appropriate for different times of day. There are devotions for mealtime, bath time, bedtime, playtime, laundry day, and anytime you'd like to make a spiritual point to your preschooler.

Just as Mary taught Jesus using the Scriptures, nature, and stories of God's providence, this book contains devotions, nature nuggets, Bible stories, examples of God's

many gifts to us, and activities built around forming and practicing good health habits.

Most of these devotions are activity based. That's because your preschooler is also activity based. It's also because educational research shows that while we remember only 10 percent of what we hear, we remember 90 percent of what we do.

You won't find a new devotion every day. That's because your preschooler loves repetition. He has a favorite story that must be repeated every night for weeks on end. Or she sings the same song over and over again. In this book we present some stories several different times in several different ways. That's to satisfy your child's need for repetition without causing terminal boredom to the rest of the family.

Since your child is unique, don't be afraid to adapt. Use your own creativity and knowledge of your child to focus these devotions to their current interest and level of understanding.

Often it is difficult to have on hand the exact craft items called for in an activity. The index grid should help you with your planning and shopping. Materials are divided as follows: your child's own toys, household items, stationery items, and craft items.

Your child's own toys include: stuffed animals, blocks, plastic animals, lizards, frogs, and bugs. Also needed is a good nature book with pictures of animals, birds, fish, insects, reptiles, and sea animals.

Household items include: laundry baskets, towels, blankets, dishes, paper plates and cups, newspaper, cookie cutters, cotton balls, cinnamon, food coloring, Band-Aids, and sponges, as well as dish soap and common food items, such as dried beans, macaroni, etc.

Stationery items include: old magazines for cutting up, scissors, construction paper, glue, stapler, pencils, markers (washable and permanent), clear tape, paper clips, and crayons.

Craft items to keep on hand include: nature stickers, pipe cleaners, a box of Popsicle sticks, and colored yarns (including green).

Prayer is an important part of devotions, and each activity should end with a short talk with God. Often a single sentence prayer is included at the end of a devotion to help you.

Not only should you and your child have fun with these activities but you will be preparing your little one for ministry. You will often hear the stories being repeated to your child's friends who come over to play. Nobody is ever too young to witness!

Enjoy helping your child get to know God as a special friend!

My Backbone

Materials: *several spools of thread, a piece of string*

J esus knew your back needed to be strong to hold the rest of your body up. So He made a backbone for you. But if Jesus had put only one bone in your back you wouldn't be able to bend over and touch your toes or bend over sideways. You wouldn't be able to stretch. You would just have to be still. When you bend forward . . . or sideways . . . you can stretch because your backbone is actually many small bones, all connected together with a cord like this:

[Help the child thread cord through several spools. Tie a knot on each end or fasten with tape. Then show the child how the column of spools can be bent slightly from side to side, though it still stays somewhat upright and cannot be bent in half.]

Your backbone is something like this. There are several little bones. You can feel each one. We have a cord that runs up the middle too. We call it our spinal cord. It goes all the way to our head.

[Since it's difficult to feel one's own backbone, allow the child to feel your backbone.]

Thank You, Jesus, for making my backbone so I can stand up straight. And thank You for making it flexible so I can bend. Amen.

#1

Theme: Healthy Body

Abel

Abel was Adam and Eve's second boy. He was Cain's little brother. Cain worked in the garden and grew food for his family. Abel was a shepherd. He would take them to places where they could get good green grass to eat. Then he would take them to a river where they could get water to drink. Abel knew that his sheep were afraid of a river if the water was moving too fast, so he always made sure they could drink from a nice quiet pool of water.

[Have the child try to drink from a hose that is on full blast, then from water trick-ling into a cup.] It is easier to drink from still water, isn't it?

Abel took good care of his animals. God is happy when we are kind to our animals. *[If you have a pet, help your child put out its food and water. If you have no pet, place dishes out anyway and pretend.]* Animals need food and water every day, just like people do. God wants us to take care of our animals just like Abel took care of his sheep and just like He takes care of us.

Dear Jesus, thank You for taking such good care of me. Amen.

Theme: God's Word

#2

The First Fight

Cain and Abel were brothers. Cain and Abel played nicely together and loved each other—most of the time. One day Cain became very angry with Abel about something.

We are going to do some pretending. I'll pretend to be Abel, and you pretend to be Cain. When you are pretending, you only *pretend* to do things. In this story you will give only a *pretend* hit.

Cain and Abel got in a fight, and Cain hit Abel very hard. *[Have Abel fall down and not move or respond for a few moments.]* It hurt Abel so badly that he died. Now Cain was sad. Cain's mom and dad were sad. God was sad. Cain didn't have a brother anymore. His brother was dead.

Usually, when you fight with a brother or a sister, nobody dies. But it makes your brother or sister sad when they get hurt from fighting. It can make you sad, too. Mom and Dad don't like it either, and it makes God sad.

Dear God, help me to play nicely and to be kind so I don't make You sad. Amen.

#3

Theme: God's Word

The Tower of Babel

Materials: *blocks*

After the Flood some of Noah's children's children forgot God. They decided to build a very tall tower so that if God sent another flood, they would run and hide in the top of the tower. This made God sad. He had already promised to never destroy the world again by a flood. The people didn't want to leave Babel, and they kept working on their tower. *[Using blocks, help the child build a tower as tall as he/she can.]*

God had a plan that would make people move to other parts of the world. When God's plan went into action, suddenly people couldn't understand each other anymore—they no longer spoke the same language. Then God sent lightning and broke the tall tower down. *[Let the child break his/her tower down.]* The people gave up trying to build the tower. When a group of people discovered they could understand each other, they moved away to a place where they could be by themselves. And this is how God got people to live all over the world.

Dear God, please help me to trust You and believe what You say. Amen.

Theme: God's Word

#4

Abraham and Lot

Materials: *two large sheets*

The Bible tells many stories about Abraham. Abraham had a nephew named Lot. Lot was a grown-up nephew, and both Abraham and Lot had big families and many servants. Abraham and Lot had a problem: Abraham's family and Lot's servants were fighting. Finally they decided that the best way to handle it was to live apart from each other. So Abraham set up his tents in one place, and Lot set up *his* tents in another place.

[Use two large sheets to make separate tents. Make them as far apart in the room as possible, draping sheets over furniture. Allow the child to sit in one tent, and other children, or yourself, to sit in the other tent.]

God is happy when we get along well with each other. But if we have problems, it is better to play in separate places than to fight. God does not want His children to fight with each other.

Dear God, help me to get along with people. But if I can't, help me to go farther away so that I won't fight. Amen.

#5

Theme: God's Word

Baby Giraffes

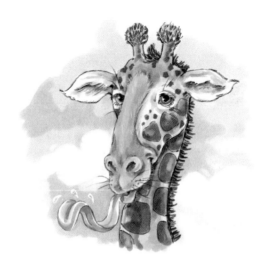

Materials: *green leaves from a tree, a bowl, dishwashing liquid*

Michael and his brother and their mom went to the zoo. They were watching the new baby giraffe drink some milk from its mommy. Then it wobbled over to the fence where they were standing and stretched out its neck.

"Come on, little one," said Mama in a soft voice. "Stick your little face over here, and I'll pet your nose." Suddenly the baby lunged toward Mama and wrapped its long, very slimy tongue around Mama's face. Then it jumped back and ran to its mommy. Mama's glasses and hat were inside the cage now. The zookeeper had to get Mama's glasses back.

The little giraffe's tongue is sticky so that the tree leaves it likes to eat will stick to its tongue when it tries to eat them. *[Rub a thick layer of dishwashing liquid on the child's arm. Have the child stick his/her arm in the bowl of leaves. Notice how the leaves stick to the slime.]*

Jesus made the baby giraffe's tongue long and sticky so it can get the leaves it needs.

Dear Jesus, You are so smart, and You made each animal just right. Amen.

Theme: Nature

#6

Elephants

Materials: *picture of elephant*

Donnie and Michael were at the zoo with their mama. They were looking at the elephants. *[Show the child a picture of an elephant.]*

"I feel sorry for the elephant," said Donnie. "If I had round flat feet on the end of my arms, I wouldn't be able to scratch my nose or pick up my sandwich or do anything."

"That's true," Mama agreed. "But God loved the elephant and gave it something that you don't have. Look at the elephant's nose. It's called a trunk, and the elephant uses it for breathing. But the elephant can also use its trunk to pick things up like you do with your hands." *[Tell the child to try to pick up something with his/her nose.]*

"Oh," said Donnie, "so God sort of did give the elephant a hand. He just put it on the end of its nose! But I'm glad He put my hands on my wrists and not on the front of my face. I would look funny!"

"Yes," laughed Mama, "but God knew that it would look just right on the elephant."

Thank You, God, for caring about the elephant and giving it a trunk. Amen.

Theme: Nature

Sticker Fun

Materials: *animal stickers, paper*

P lace three different animal stickers on a sheet of paper and three duplicate stickers in different places on the same piece of paper. Help the child match the animals and draw lines between the matching pairs. For a more advanced child, give more stickers to choose from or add an extra one that does not match and have the child find the one that does not fit.]

When God called the animals to come into Noah's ark, many of them came in two by two. Let's help these animals find their mates so they can go to Noah's ark.

Thank You, Jesus, for keeping the animals safe in the ark. Amen.

Theme: Nature

Counting the Animals

Materials: *animal stickers, paper*

On one sheet of paper, have the child place one animal sticker; on the second sheet, two stickers; and on the third sheet, three stickers.]

God gave Adam a special job. He was to give names to each animal. Adam counted the animals too.

How many animals are on this page? How many on this one? *[As you count each animal, place the child's finger on the animal. If your child does not know how to count or does not know the names of the animals, three animals is enough.]*

What is the name of this kind of animal? *[If your child is more advanced and can count further than three or already knows animal names, add as many pages as are necessary, or purchase stickers of some less common animals. Punch holes in the papers and allow the child to add animal pages to his/her notebook and return to count and name them whenever he/she wishes. For a more advanced preschooler, this activity can be adapted for birds and flowers, too.]*

Thank You, Jesus, for all the animals and for making each one special. Amen.

Theme: Nature

Naming the Animals

Materials: *animal stickers of pets, farm and zoo animals; paper, pencil*

U sing stickers of well-known animals such as pets, farm animals, or zoo animals, allow the child to place one sticker of each animal on the page. Then point to each animal and name it. Have the child point and name the animal after you. Each animal the child names correctly becomes his/hers. Have the child draw a circle around it until all the animals have been circled.]

One of the jobs God gave Adam was to name the animals. See how many of these animals you can name.

Dear Jesus, please help me to love and care for the animals You made for me to enjoy. Amen.

Theme: Nature

#10

Animal Dominoes

Materials: *3" x 5" cards, animal stickers*

Make a set of animal dominoes, using 3" x 5" cards. Draw a line down the middle of each card, making two almost-square sections (3" x 2½"). Then allow the child to place an animal sticker at either end of the card. Be sure there are at least two—and preferably four—of each animal somewhere in the stack of cards. Match up the cards, end to end, domino style, until all the cards have been used.]

Dear Jesus, how did You ever think of so many wonderful animals to make? Thank You for each one! Amen.

Theme: Nature

Paul Escapes

Materials: *laundry basket, rope or belt*

If a laundry basket and rope are not available, you may use a small basket and a doll that fits in the basket, or a disposable cup with a pipe cleaner handle and a pipe cleaner man in the cup.]

Paul had gone to a city to tell people about Jesus. But there were some bad men who lived in that city who didn't want anyone to hear about Jesus. They planned to catch Paul and kill him.

Paul's friends heard about it before the bad men got there. So they put Paul in a basket and gently lowered him down over the side of the city wall. *[Place your child in the laundry basket and gently lower it over the side of the chair till it rests on the floor. Then say, "Run away and hide! Don't let the bad man catch you!"]*

Jesus was so good to give Paul friends who cared about him and who helped him escape. Jesus is good to give us friends, too.

Thank You, Jesus, for my friends who are kind and helpful. Amen.

Theme: God's Word

#12

Jacob's Family Promise

Materials: *play jewelry, "idols," large bowl, sand*

H*elp the children bury jewelry and idols in the sand.]*
Jacob loved God. He had a very large family. He had four wives, 12 sons, and a daughter. Jacob loved God, and he taught his family to love God, but some of them had brought their idols along with them.

Jacob was very sad. He told his family about how much God loved them. They decided to show God how much they loved Him by burying all their idols. To show what a special occasion it was, they took off all their jewelry. The Bible says they took off their earrings and bracelets and buried them all, just like their idols.

God wants us to choose to love Him too.

Dear God, we love You so much, just as Jacob's family did. Amen.

Theme: God's Word

Whales' Spouts

Materials: *a balloon, a picture of a whale*

*T*his devotional is best done in the bathtub.]
Whales look a little like very big fish, but they aren't. Fish breathe water through their gills. Whales breathe air, as you and I do. Take a big breath of air. The air goes in through your nose. Whales breathe through a hole on top of their head called a blowhole. Whales can hold their breath and swim underwater for a long time, but they have to come up to the top of the water to breathe.

You let the air out from your last breath before you take in new air. So does the whale. *[Blow up a balloon, but do not tie it in a knot. Hold the balloon underwater.]* We'll pretend this balloon is the whale's lung. When it's ready to let its air out, it lets go. *[Let go of the balloon enough so that it blows the air up through the water, making a little fountain.]* When the whale does this, it makes some water shoot up into the air in a spout of water.

Thank You, God, for making each of Your creatures exactly right. Amen.

Theme: Nature

#14

Guardian Angels

Materials: *facial tissue, Tootsie Pop candy sucker, yarn, pipe cleaner*

God knew we would sometimes need help and protection. So He sent angels to help us. We can't see angels—they are invisible. But they are all around us. Each one of us has a guardian angel whom God sent to take care of us. Even though we can't see them, we know they are there.

[Make an angel by completely opening up a tissue and spreading it over a Tootsie Pop candy sucker. Tie the yarn snugly around the angel's neck, right below the head of the pop. Use the ends of the tissue to make wings. If no pipe cleaners are available, tie with yarn and then Scotch-tape cutout paper wings on the back of the angel. You may want to stand your angels in a little Styrofoam block or hang them from a mobile or little tree branch in your child's room to remind him/her that angels are watching over him/her all the time.]

Dear God, thank You for sending angels to watch over me. Amen.

Theme: Angels

Watermelon T-shirt

Materials: *white T-shirt (child size); newspaper; red, green, and black acrylic paint; slice of watermelon*

I'm so glad God made watermelon! It is green on the outside, but when we cut it open *[cut watermelon]*, it is red and juicy on the inside. The green outside protects the watermelon and keeps it fresh and juicy until we are ready to eat it.

The little black spots are seeds. God put the seeds in the watermelon so that after we eat it the seeds can be planted to grow more watermelons.

[Fold the newspaper and place it inside the shirt to keep paint from soaking through to the other side. Around the collar of the shirt, mark a wide semicircle, going from one shoulder to the other. Have the child fill in the area with red paint. If your child is an advanced preschooler, allow him/her to leave a little white space and paint a green border around it for the rind. Help the child make a few dark spots in the red part for seeds. Allow the shirt to dry 24 hours before wearing.]

Thank You, Jesus, for making watermelons, and thank You for helping me with my picture so I can remember what the watermelon was like, even when it's all gone. Amen.

Theme: Nature

#16

Reverence

Materials: *wax paper, several broken crayons, dish towel, an iron*

Place one sheet of wax paper on the table. Let the child break up crayons into tiny pieces or help him/her by using a knife or a vegetable peeler. When the child has the colored shavings arranged the way he/she likes them, place a second sheet of wax paper over the first. Cover with a dish towel and press with a hot iron. The result is a translucent "stained-glass window." You may tape this to your child's window so that the light can shine through it. A way to make it last longer would be to make a cardboard frame around the edges and attach it to the wax paper to protect the edges.]*

When we are in church, we are in God's house. Often churches have pretty things, like pretty colored windows, that help us remember it is God's house. But we can be in God's presence anytime we talk to Him.

Making a stained-glassed window helps remind us that we are in God's presence anytime we talk to Him.

Thank You, God, for being with me any time I talk to You, even when I'm not in church. Amen.

Theme: Being Reverent

Emergencies

Materials: *telephone, paper, crayons*

S ometimes we have accidents or hurt ourselves. Sometimes houses catch on fire. It is good to know what to do to get help in an emergency.

[Teach your child how to dial 911. On a sheet of paper, draw the phone buttons with large numbers on them. Have your child color the 9 and the 1 in bright colors to show that these are the buttons one pushes in an emergency.] When you push these numbers, another adult will come and help you. Use these numbers only if it is an emergency and someone is hurt or the house is on fire

or you are afraid, and there is no adult to help you.

Talking to God is like talking on the phone except we can call Him anytime. The people who answer when we dial 911 would not be happy if you called them just to tell them about what you had done that day. But God loves to hear about your pets and your friends and anything you want to talk to Him about.

Thank You, God, for being willing to talk to me anytime, even when there is no emergency. Amen.

Theme: Prayer

#18

Nature T-shirt

Materials: T-shirt (child's size), paper bag, leaves, shells and treasures found on the beach, can of spray paint appropriate for fabric

This activity is especially effective for hand-me-down T-shirts. The night before the activity, place a folded paper bag inside the shirt so paint doesn't soak through and spray paint of a contrasting color to cover original design on T-shirt. This makes the child feel he/she has a new shirt instead of an old hand-me-down.

[Precede this activity with a walk so that the child can collect leaves, ferns, or flowers for the activity. Fold a paper bag and place it inside the T-shirt so paint doesn't soak through to the other side. Have the child arrange two or three of his/her favorite collected items on the T-shirt, then spray with spray paint. Pull the items off so the child can see the silhouettes of the objects he/she chose. Allow the shirt to dry 24 hours before wearing.]

Thank You, God, for helping me find such neat things on my walk today. Amen.

Theme: Nature

Nature Quilt Hanging

Materials: *four, nine, or 12 squares of adhesive-backed felt with a peel-off backing; backing fabric*

Arrange quilt-style; measure and cut fabric backing to size. Take the child for a walk to collect leaves, flowers, shells, or other nature items for the quilt design. Place the felt square on newspaper. Have the child arrange nature item or items on the square. Spray with spray paint, then remove the nature items. This activity also can be done by dipping the child's hand in paint and making handprints on each quilt square. More advanced children may want to paint their own picture on each quilt square or use stencils.

[Repeat with each quilt square. Allow to dry. The next day, help the child peel paper backing off the felt and arrange squares on the fabric quilt-back piece. Receiving blankets and the child's old baby blankets are useful for quilt backings. Trim the edges. The quilt can be used as your child's own personal quilt, a wall hanging, or a gift for grandparents.]

Dear Jesus, thank You for making such pretty things outside. Every time I look at my quilt, help me to remember how much You love me. Amen.

Theme: Nature

#20

Colors

Materials: *water, food coloring in primary colors*

On the first day of Creation, God made light. On this day God made colors, too, for all colors are made of light. God made many different kinds of light and color. Today we're going to learn some special secrets about the colors God made.

[Put a drop of red food coloring in the cup of water. Let the child stir it with a straw or a spoon.] What color is this? That's right. It's red. God made the color red on the first day.

[In another cup, drop two drops of yellow food coloring. Have the child stir.] What color is this? That's right. It's yellow.

[Now have the child pour a cup of red and a cup of yellow together into a larger container.] What color is it now? That's right. God used red and yellow to make orange when they are mixed together.

Let's try another color. *[Repeat the experiment with red plus blue, and blue plus yellow. For the most effective demonstration, remember that it takes more yellow than red or blue because it's a lighter color.]*

Thank You, God, for making such beautiful colors for our world. And thank You for helping me learn about the secrets of how colors are made. Amen.

Theme: Creation

My Soul, Part 1

Materials: *mirror, flashlight*

When people at church talk about your soul, they're talking about the part of your mind that decides whether or not you want to love Jesus. Your soul is a little like this mirror. *[Shine the flashlight on the mirror.]* When you shine the light on the mirror, you can reflect it. Although the mirror doesn't have any light inside itself, it can reflect the light from the flashlight. Our souls are just like that. We don't have any goodness inside of us, but when we love Jesus, we reflect His love just like the mirror reflects the light. What happens when you turn away from the flashlight? *[Have the child turn the mirror away.]* Can you reflect light now?

It's just like that with Jesus. As long as we're thinking about Jesus with our mind, we'll reflect His love to other people. But if our soul turns away from Jesus—not thinking about Jesus and not loving Him anymore—then we don't reflect His love anymore.

[Have the child turn the mirror back to the light so he/she can reflect it again.]

Dear Jesus, help me always to love You so that I can reflect like this mirror. Amen.

Theme: My Soul

#22

My Soul, Part 2

Materials: *mirror, flashlight, shaving cream*

Looking at Jesus and thinking about Him is important in order for us to be able to reflect His love to other people. But something else is important too. *[Shine the light on the mirror and have the child reflect the light.]* Our souls can reflect Jesus' light and Jesus' love only when they are nice and clean.

[Spray a small amount of shaving cream on the mirror. Have the child reflect the light now.] What happens to the reflected light? Is there as much?

[Now spray shaving cream and smear all over the mirror so the surface is completely covered.] What about now? Even though the mirror is looking toward the light, it can't reflect any. Why not?

We need to keep our souls clean, too, or our souls will not be able to reflect Jesus' light. We can clean the mirror by wiping it off with a paper towel. But our souls are inside our minds. How do we clean that? We just ask Jesus.

Jesus, please make my soul nice and clean. Take away anything that would keep me from reflecting Your love. Amen. [Help child repeat prayer.]

Theme: My Soul

Better Than Bears

Materials: *a teddy bear or small wooden bear cutout, paint, stick-on eyes, and magnet*

*H*ave the child paint a bear, then help him/her glue on eyes and put a magnet on the back so that the bear can stick to the fridge.]

Many people love teddy bears. They are fun to play with. They are fun to snuggle with in bed at night while you sleep. You can whisper your secret in your teddy bear's ear, and it never tells anybody. Some people feel as though their teddy bear is their best friend. But there is a Friend who is even better than your teddy bear. It's God.

You can take God to bed with you at night, too. You can talk to Him from your little bed, and He will hear you and listen to all your secrets and everything you tell Him. He will stay near you all night and watch over you and keep you safe. And He never tells any of your secrets, either.

But God is better than a bear. God is *real*. He can think. He can remember. And He can help you with your problems and the things you are afraid of. Teddy bears are wonderful, but God is even better.

Dear God, I love You even more than my teddy bear. Amen.

Theme: Prayer

#24

Thanks Mobile

Materials: *several small wooden cutout shapes*

Try to buy shapes that can be painted all one color, such as a tree, cow, and goose. The goose and cow can be painted solid white, adding a dot for eyes. The tree shape can be painted solid green. This is especially important for younger painters who lack the fine motor controls to paint details. The child can paint all of these shapes in one day and hang them from a coat hanger by threads, or you can do one shape a day. As you hang the shape from the coat hanger, pray a thank-You prayer to God for creating each item.]

Theme: Thankfulness

Recycling

Materials: *an old vinyl long-playing record*

Wasting means throwing away something that could be used. Recycling is when we save something that has already been used and make it into something else we can use again.

This record used to go on a record player to play music like we hear on CDs and cassette tapes now. Most people don't have record players anymore, so we're going to use it to make something else.

[Turn a Pyrex bowl upside down on a cookie sheet. Set the record on top of it and place it in a 200 °F oven. Peek in the oven every five minutes. As the record gets hot the vinyl will get soft and droop down over the bowl. When this happens, carefully remove the cookie sheet, bowl, and record from the oven. When it is cool, take it off the bowl and turn it right side up. Use enamel spray paint and spray the bowl inside and out, then allow the child to paint designs on it. When the bowl is dry, place a napkin in it and allow the child to serve rolls or chips in it. Use often and allow the child to tell others about recycling.]*

Dear Jesus, thank You for giving us good ideas for using things again. Amen.

Theme: Stewardship

#26

Saving Leftovers

Materials: *plastic bags or containers*

Tthis devotional is best done while cleaning up after a meal. Help child put leftovers into containers and place in refrigerator.]

Big crowds would often come to hear Jesus speak. One day Jesus told stories all day long. The people hadn't had any lunch. By evening they were very hungry. Using a little boy's lunch, Jesus did a miracle. He kept breaking the food into smaller and smaller pieces—and still there was more! He fed the whole crowd of 5,000 people with one little boy's lunch!

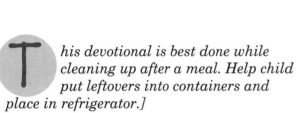

Then Jesus said something important after everyone had eaten. He sent His disciples around with baskets to pick up all the leftovers so that nothing would be wasted. The leftover food was shared with poor people who didn't have enough food to eat. We save our leftover food and eat it later. Perhaps we will warm this up for supper or eat it tomorrow. It pleases Jesus when we don't waste anything.

Dear Jesus, please help me to learn not to waste anything. Amen.

#27

Theme: Stewardship

A Squirrel's Tail

Material: *picture of squirrel*

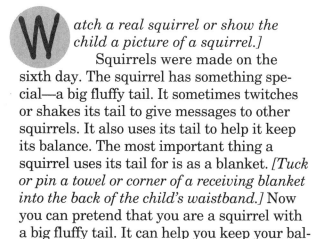

Watch *a real squirrel or show the child a picture of a squirrel.]*
Squirrels were made on the sixth day. The squirrel has something special—a big fluffy tail. It sometimes twitches or shakes its tail to give messages to other squirrels. It also uses its tail to help it keep its balance. The most important thing a squirrel uses its tail for is as a blanket. *[Tuck or pin a towel or corner of a receiving blanket into the back of the child's waistband.]* Now you can pretend that you are a squirrel with a big fluffy tail. It can help you keep your balance while you run around. *[Have the child run.]* But the most important thing is that your tail can keep you warm. You can pull your fluffy tail up over yourself like a little blanket, and it will keep you warm.

Jesus knew that squirrels would need a blanket when they hibernate (that means sleep during cold weather), so He gave them big, fluffy tails. God thinks of everything. He is so good!

Dear God, thank You for giving the squirrel a fluffy tail. And thank You for giving me a blanket instead. Amen.

Theme: Nature

#28

Bears

Materials: *piece of furry fabric or real fur, picture of bear*

S*how the child a picture of a bear or go to the zoo and see a bear.]* You have a head with eyes, nose, ears, and mouth, just like the bear. You have a body. So does the bear. You have arms and legs. So does the bear. What is different? The bear has a little tail. You don't have a tail. But the bear has something else. The bear is furry all over. If you could pet a bear, you would find its fur to be thick and fluffy and very warm. We can't pet bears here on earth because they are wild, and they would bite us. But in heaven we will be able to pet a bear.

Jesus knew that bears would need to stay warm in cold weather. Bears hibernate—which means they sleep—all winter. God gave the bear fur. The bear wears its furry blanket all the time. This keeps it nice and warm in the winter. Whether it is awake or whether it is asleep, the bear is cozy and comfortable, just as you are under your blanket in your bed at night.

Dear Jesus, thank You for making the bears furry so they can be warm, and thank You for my blanket. Amen.

#29

Theme: Nature

Birds Fly South

Materials: *popsicle stick, construction paper*

Fold construction paper. Cut a long triangle, the fold being the short base. Put white glue in the fold and place it in the middle of the popsicle stick. Then fold wings out so that when the stick is waved up and down, the wings flap. Have the child draw an eye at one end of the popsicle stick. Add the beak, if desired.]

Not all animals hibernate, or sleep, through the winter. Some birds leave and go to warmer places. When the cold weather is coming, they gather in big groups and fly south. We call this migrating. They fly a long way until they are at the right place for them to stay until the weather is warmer again. Then they fly all the way back.

Birds that migrate don't have maps. They don't have cars or airplanes to travel in, yet they know exactly where to go and exactly where to come back. Jesus knew which birds could live here all winter long, and which ones need to go to a warmer place. Isn't He wonderful!

Dear Jesus, You are so smart! And You help all the birds know exactly what to do. You are awesome! Amen.

Theme: Nature

HFJ-4

#30

Triangles

Materials: *paper, toothpicks, crayons*

od used all kinds of interesting shapes when He made our world. A triangle is a shape that has three sides and three pointed corners. *[Draw a triangle on a piece of paper, then give the child three toothpicks. Place them in a triangle shape.]*

Can you think of anything God made that is in a triangle shape? *[Draw three large triangles on a piece of paper. Make one wider at the bottom than the others. Color one triangle dark green and give it a brown trunk.]* What is this one? Yes, it's a pine tree.

[Have the child color the second triangle orange, and then draw little sprigs of green from its base.] What's this? Yes, this is a carrot.

[Have the child color the third triangle red, then add a green rim across the base of it and draw black dots on it for seeds.] What does this look like? Yes, it's a piece of watermelon.

All three of these are triangle shapes. They have three sides and three pointed corners. Our world would be very boring if everything were all the same shape.

Thank You, God, for making triangle shapes. Amen.

Theme: Shapes

Triangle Lunch

Materials: *fruit, bread*

I'm so glad that God made triangle shapes, aren't you? We're going to have a triangle snack for lunch. *[Serve triangular shapes of watermelon. Cut wedges of apple, then slice crossways so that apple pieces are in triangles. This can be done with oranges, also. Cut triangle bread and make little triangle sandwiches.]*

Thank You, God, for triangles, and thank You for my triangle lunch. Amen.

Theme: Shapes

#32

Inside Secrets

Materials: *fruit, paper*

God hid pretty secrets inside many of the different fruits and vegetables that He made. Let's find out what's inside.

[Use apple, orange, melon, banana, potato, and any other fruit you have available. Slice cross sections of all of them and allow the child to examine them.]

The inside of a potato is just plain, but look at the pretty shapes inside the apple and the orange.

[Pour some paint into a small plate. Allow the child to place the sliced fruit or vegetable, sliced surface down, in the paint. Then use as a stamp on paper to have a permanent record of the different cross-section pictures.]

Thank You, God, for making such pretty inside secrets in the food that You made for us. Amen.

#33

Theme: Shapes

My Hands

Materials: *crayons, paper*

Our hands look very much like each other, but they are different. On your left hand your thumb is on one side of your hand, while on your right hand your thumb is on the other side. *[Put a different colored dot on your child's left and right hand.]* This is your left hand. This is your right hand. We call them "left" and "right" to tell them apart. Everybody's hand on this side is called "right." Everybody's hand on this side is called "left."

Clench your fists really tight and squeeze hard. Which hand is stronger? Both hands are probably about the same. But we don't use them the same. Use a spoon and try and to eat spoonfuls of water with each hand. See which hand is the easiest. Now color with a crayon. Which hand colors the best? Some people's right hand colors the best. We call them "right-handed." Other people's left hand colors the best, and we call them "left-handed," but either one is OK. There are many things we do that we need both hands for.

Thank You, Jesus, for my right hand and my left hand. Amen.

Theme: Left and Right

#34

Frogs' Tongues

Materials: *mirror, rubber band*

Have the child stick his/her tongue out.] Look at your tongue in the mirror. What shape is your tongue? A frog's tongue is long and skinny and stretchy like this rubber band. It can stretch out long and then come back and be short again. Can your tongue do that? No. Our tongues can stretch only a little bit.

Frogs' tongues are different because of what they eat. Frogs eat bugs. When a little bug flies by, the frog can stretch its tongue way out and grab the bug and pull it into its mouth. The frog has a sticky pad on the end of its tongue that sticks to the bug so it can't get away. Do you have a sticky pad on the end of your tongue? No. This is because God didn't plan for you to eat bugs. Your tongue is small and rounder and wet, not sticky. It stays inside your mouth because God knew just what kind of food you would eat and just what kind of food the frogs would eat. God was so wise.

Dear God, thank You for giving the frog a stretchy tongue so it can catch bugs. And thank You for giving me a little round tongue and for not making me eat bugs. Amen.

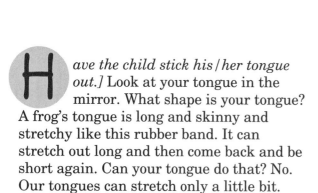
#35

Theme: Nature

Jellyfish

Materials: *round bowl, cooking spray, flavored gelatin, several strands of cooked spaghetti*

The jellyfish is a very funny animal that lives in the ocean, as fish do. But it's made differently. It has no bones. It's just a little blob of jiggly jelly. Most jellyfish have long, stringy things hanging down underneath them called "tentacles." The jellyfish uses these to catch food.

Sometimes after it rains, you can find jellyfish washed up on the beach. But people should never pick up jellyfish on the beach, not even dead ones. Do you know why? Many jellyfish have stingers in their tentacles.

[Spray a round bowl with nonstick cooking spray. Have the child help you drape the spaghetti "tentacles" over the sides of the bowl, leaving about half of each tentacle inside the round bowl. Mix gelatin with only half the water called for, and then pour it into the bowl. Place the entire jellyfish mixture in the refrigerator. When set, dip the bowl in warm water and turn it upside down on a plate. The jellyfish should slide right out of the bowl. Let the child touch it.]

Thank You, God, for making so many different kinds of animals. You are so smart! Amen.

Theme: Nature

#36

Cats' Paws

Materials: *cat (tame and wild) pictures*

There are small cats we keep as pets, and there are bigger cats, like lions and tigers. *[Look at pictures of domestic cats, cougars, lions, and tigers.]* The big cats have big claws. *[Pretend your fingers are big claws.]* You couldn't play with them without getting hurt. Their claws are there all the time. They use them for catching and tearing up their food.

Pet cats have soft little paws. They have claws, too, but they hide them inside their paws, so you can play with them without getting scratched. *[Hide your finger "claws"* inside your hand.]* When pet cats need to protect themselves, God made their claws so they can come back out. *[Open your finger "claws" and pull them out again.]* But as soon as they are ready to be gentle again, they pull their claws back into their paws. *[Put your "claws" away.]*

God thought of everything when He was creating the animals!

Thank You, God, for making small cats' paws the way You did, so that we can pet them and not get hurt. Amen.

Theme: Nature

Lizards

Materials: *toy lizard or a picture of a lizard*

I f possible, go to a zoo to see lizards. If that's not possible, use a toy lizard or picture of one.]

A lizard looks a little bit like a short, fat snake with arms and legs. It has dry scaly skin. Most lizards live in warm countries. They have some natural enemies. Some kinds of birds like to catch lizards and eat them. Some animals do, too. In some countries, people eat the bigger lizards, such as the iguanas.

God made a special way for lizards to escape when they are in danger. When an ani-mal or a person grabs a lizard by its tail, the tail falls off and little nerves in it make the tail wriggle and squirm and look like a snake, while the lizard is able to run away quickly and hide. God made the lizard able to grow a new tail.

God cares about all His creatures, and He gave you adults to help protect you. He also gave you a guardian angel to take care of you.

Dear Jesus, thank You for making the lizard's tail the way that it is. And thank You for providing protection for me. Amen.

Theme: Nature

#38

Opossums

Materials: *play-dough, pipe cleaners, picture of an opossum*

Michael pointed to something just inside the garage. "Is it a rat?" It was a tiny animal with a pointed little face, gray fur, and a long naked tail.

"No," Mom said. "That's an opossum. Its mama must have been hurt on the road." She scooped it up in a wastebasket. "Let's take this little fellow back to the house."

They fed the opossum formula from a doll-sized baby bottle. The baby sucked eagerly, hanging on to the bottle with both hands and feet, even wrapping its little tail tightly around it.

"Jesus made opossums special," said Mama. "He made their tails work like a hand. When the mama travels, the babies ride on her back. She holds her tail up over her back, and they all wrap their little tails around hers and hang on."

[Shape play-dough into an egg shape with a pointed little head at one end. Stick the pipe cleaner tail deep into the egg and wind it around a little bottle, or hang your opossum by the tail.]

Thank You, Jesus, for making opossums' tails so cool. Amen.

#39

Theme: Nature

The Ostrich

Materials: *picture of an ostrich, pipe cleaners, construction paper, feathers, glue*

The ostrich is the biggest bird in the world. It is taller than most grown-ups you know. Its eggs are so big that in some countries the shells are used for containers. Ostriches have very strong legs. They can kick so hard they can even defend themselves against lions. They can make a loud roaring noise with their beak and can hiss. Ostriches have very pretty feathers, too.

People used to say that when ostriches were scared they would stick their head in the sand. But this isn't true. God made the ostriches smarter than that. Instead, they usually run away.

Let's make an ostrich. *[Cut an oval from construction paper. Help the child glue lots of feathers on the oval, all going one direction. Bend a pipe cleaner in half. Help the child glue or Scotch-tape it behind the feathered body and bend the two ends to make feet. Cut another pipe cleaner in half and tape it to the body for the ostrich's neck. Bend one end to make into a triangle for the head.]*

Thank You, God, for making the big ostrich. Amen.

Theme: Nature

#40

The Owl

Materials: *paper plates, markers, two brass brads*

Most owls sleep during the day and are awake at night. They can hang on to things with their big, sharp, strong claws. Owls have a small beak and big eyes that make them look very wise and can see very well in the dark. They can't move their eyes from side to side like you do, so God made their necks special so that the owl is able to turn its head almost all the way around.

[*Cut one inch off each side of a paper plate. Draw sharp claws at the bottom or Scotch-tape on pipe cleaners that can be bent into claws. Draw a line across the top quarter of the plate. Make large eyes that take up this entire section. Then make a small beak between the eyes, right on the line. Cut a one-inch strip out of the middle of a second paper plate. Throw this piece away. Attach the two side pieces with brass brads just below the eye line on the owl so that it can flap its wings.*]

Dear God, I'm glad You made the owl's neck so that the owl can look behind itself, but thank You for giving me eyes that can move. Please make me really wise. Amen.

Theme: Nature

The Rattlesnake

Materials: *paper plates, macaroni, marker pens*

One of the poisonous snakes that live in North America is called the rattlesnake. Rattlesnakes have a rattle on the end of their tail. It looks like they have two rows of little beads sewn to the end of their tail, almost like buttons. A rattlesnake may add several buttons to its rattle each year—one for each time it sheds its skin. You can't tell a rattlesnake's age by looking at the buttons, but you know that one with lots of buttons is much older than one with only a few.

Even though a rattlesnake can hurt people, God made the rattlesnake able to give a warning. It coils and shakes its rattle. When people and animals hear this warning, it gives them a chance to get away.

[Put uncooked macaroni between two paper plates and staple the edges together. Have the child use a marker to draw a big black snake on the front of one paper plate. Then shake the plate to hear your rattlesnake rattle a warning.]

Thank You, God, for making the rattlesnake with a rattle warning on the end of its tail. Amen.

Theme: Nature

#42

The Rhinoceros

Materials: *paper cup, elastic string or yarn*

Poke a hole in either side of the paper cup and thread the string through it. Fasten behind the child's head so he/she has a big horn on the front of his/her nose.]

The rhinoceros is a big animal that lives in Africa. It has a big strong body and is covered with tough, heavy skin that's almost like armor. It has a little short tail, and a great big horn on its nose. Some kinds of rhinoceroses have two horns on their noses—a tall one in front and a shorter one right behind it.

The rhinoceros can't see very well. When it thinks it's in danger, it runs toward the sound with its head down and its horn pointing straight ahead. *[Have the child lower his/her head and run with the "horn" sticking out in front of him/her.]* The rhinoceros isn't actually as grumpy as people think it is—it just can't see very well, and so it gets upset or scared easily.

Some people are like the rhinoceros. If you get to know them, though, you find out they aren't really grumpy.

Dear Jesus, help me to be understanding of others. Amen.

Theme: Nature

#43

Flying Squirrels

Materials: *safety pins, baby-sized quilt or receiving blanket or a large towel*

F lying squirrels can't really fly. What they do is glide. Flying squirrels have a thin layer of stretchy skin on each side that stretches from the front foot to the back foot, all the way along their body. *[Use safety pins to attach the baby blanket to the back of the child's neckline. Then pin the corners of the blanket to each wrist and ankle so that when the child stretches his/her arms and legs out, the blanket is open wide.]* When they jump from branch to branch, they spread out their wings and trap the air under them so they *look* like they're flying. But they really only glide from one tree to another.

Your blanket won't make it so that you can fly, but it works for the squirrels because they're smaller. They use their tail to help steer them and to help them land with their head up so they don't bang their head on the trees when they land.

They eat nuts and fruit and seeds and actually live in holes in trees. Flying squirrels are shy and like to come out only at night.

Jesus, I can't wait till I get to heaven and can fly, too! Amen.

Theme: Nature

#44

Spiders

Materials: *fabric, Velcro dots, plastic bugs, picture of spiderweb*

*D*raw a spiderweb on the fabric. Have the child help you attach the Velcro dots to the spiderweb and the bugs. Allow the child to attach the bugs to the Velcro dots on the spiderweb so they get "caught."]

Spiders are little crawly creatures who have eight legs. Some are so tiny that you can hardly see them, and some are bigger than my hand. While it's true that some spiders can bite and hurt people, most spiders are harmless.

[Show a picture of a spiderweb if you can't find a real one to look at.] Most spiders eat bugs. God made their bodies able to make sticky threads called spider silk. They weave these into a spiderweb, and when bugs fly into the web, they stick to it because spiderwebs are sticky. Then the spider can eat the bugs.

Spiders in your garden can help eat the bugs that would hurt your plants. Like people, some spiders are good, and some are bad. But if you don't bother them, they won't bother you.

Thank You, God, for making spiders to take the harmful bugs out of our homes and gardens. Amen.

Theme: Nature

Spiderweb

Materials: *construction paper, white glue, glitter*

L ook at a spiderweb when the grass is still damp from the night before.] When the sun shines through the spiderweb, it looks sparkly. This is because little drops of water are caught in the spiderweb.

How does a spider make such a pretty thing? Let's make a spiderweb. *[Using the glue on dark construction paper, draw one line straight down the middle, then make another line straight across the middle. Now make one line from the top right corner to the bottom left corner, and another*

line from the bottom right corner to the top left corner. Starting in the middle, make a little line of glue that goes around and around until it gets to the outside edge. Dump the glitter on the paper. Allow it to sit for a minute, then hold it upside down and shake over a wastebasket. The extra glitter will fall off, revealing a spiderweb that looks sparkly and pretty, just like an early morning spiderweb from the garden.]

Dear God, thank You for teaching the spiders to make such pretty things. Amen.

Theme: Nature

Devotion

#46

Baby Spiders

Materials: *small plastic spiders, yarn, pushpin tacks*

Spiders lay very tiny eggs. They climb to a high place, often on the side of your house, and spin a little cocoon out of their spider silk and hide their eggs inside. The baby spiders grow inside the egg until it's time for them to hatch. They break out of the egg but stay inside the cocoon until they grow a little bigger. When they finally break out of the cocoon, they look just like their mother, except they are very tiny. Then the wind blows them away, and they are spread over the country-side, sometimes hundreds of miles away.

[Plastic spider rings, available at Halloween, are excellent for this activity. Place eight tacks in a circle on a bulletin board. Wrap the yarn around them until the yarn lines go to each compass point. Cut off a long segment of yarn and weave it in and out, from the center, until you've created a large yarn spiderweb. Using the little ring backs on the spider rings, loop them around the spiderweb and hang spider babies on the web.]

Dear Jesus, You make such neat ways for the baby spiders to go to all the places that need them. You are so smart! Amen.

#47

Theme: Nature

Stinky Skunks

Materials: *picture of skunk, perfume*

Skunks are little black-and-white furry animals with big fluffy tails. They look very snuggly and cuddly, but they aren't. Skunks have sharp claws and sharp teeth, and they don't like to be picked up. But that isn't what people notice first. Skunks smell bad, so bad you can smell them before they get very close to you.

Why would Jesus make an animal smell bad? It's the skunk's protection. When bigger animals try to attack a skunk, it lifts its tail in the air and sprays such terrible smelling spray that the attacking animal runs away.

You don't smell bad. God made you smell good. *[Spray some perfume on the child's wrist.]* Sometimes people put on perfume to make them smell even nicer. God knew you had other ways to be protected. He gave you parents who love you and a guardian angel to watch over you, so you didn't need a bad smell. Aren't you glad!

Dear Jesus, thank You for giving protection to the little skunks, but thank You for making me the way I am and making me smell good. Amen.

Theme: Nature

#48

Postage

Materials: *envelopes*

*H*ave the child color a picture for Grandma or other appreciative family friend. Place it in an envelope. Allow the child to lick the envelope and help address it.]

When we want to send a picture to someone we love, we put it in an envelope with a stamp on it. That way, the mail carrier knows we've paid money for him/her to carry our letter to the person we addressed it to. This envelope has your picture for Grandma in it.

[Place an X in the corner of the envelope where the stamp should go. Give the child a stamp to stick over the X on the envelope. Then walk together to the mailbox and mail it.] Now that we have put the stamp on, we know your letter will get to Grandma. In a few days we can call her and see how she liked your picture.

When we send a message to God, it doesn't need a stamp. All we have to do is close our eyes and talk to Him. He'll always hear us right away.

Dear Jesus, thank You that I'm able to send a message to You anytime. Amen.

#49

Theme: Prayer

Up and Down

his devotional is appropriate once your child has learned the concept of up and down.]

We are going to have a pointing quiz. With each thing we mention we need to point up if that thing is up, and down if that thing is down. Ready?

    Grass
    The sky
    Stones
    Flowers
    Clouds
    Earth
    Sunshine
    Knee
    Jesus

That's right. Jesus is up in heaven, and we are down here on the earth. But someday Jesus is going to come back and get us. Then we can be in heaven with Him. I can't wait till that happens, can you?

Dear Jesus, we're excited that You're coming to take us home someday. Then we can be with You. Amen.

Theme: Second Coming

#50

Devotion

Body Parts

U *se the child's name as you point to each body part.]*
Jesus made *Vanessa's* hair. Jesus made *Vanessa's* nose. Thank You, Jesus, for making *Vanessa's* hair, and thank You, Jesus, for making her nose.

Jesus made *Vanessa's* ears—right ear, left ear. Thank You, Jesus, for making *Vanessa's* ears.

Jesus made *Vanessa's* lips. Thank You, Jesus, for making *Vanessa's* lips.

Jesus made *Vanessa's* chin. Thank You, Jesus, for making *Vanessa's* chin.

Jesus made *Vanessa's* fingers. Thank You, Jesus, for making *Vanessa's* fingers, etc.

[Then ask the child to point to each part, or if they already know all their parts, to name each one as you point to it. It can generate great merriment for the older preschooler to identify a body part incorrectly and allow the child to decide if you are right or wrong and give the correct answer.]

#51

Theme: God Made Me

Snack Time

Use the child's name to fill in the blanks.]
_____ is hungry. It's time for a snack or a drink of juice. Jesus knew that _____ would get hungry often. That's why Jesus made sure that _____'s mommy and daddy would have everything they would need so they could give him/her food when he/she was hungry.

[If your preschooler is older, have him/her name each item on the plate and mention each item in their prayer of thanks.]

Thank You, Jesus, for good things to eat and drink. Amen.

Theme: Thankfulness

#52

Time for a Change

Many preschoolers still have occasional problems with bed-wetting and potty training. While this can be frustrating to all involved, it's important for them to know that Jesus doesn't get mad at them for their wetting accidents. He knows these things happen and has provided for them.]

Uh-oh! It's time for a change. Jesus knew that until boys and girls were big enough to go potty by themselves all the time, they would need changes. We like to get changed as soon as we are wet or dirty so we can keep clean and fresh. Jesus wants us to stay clean and fresh so we don't get sore or sick. That would make Him feel sad for us! That's why Jesus made sure that Mommy and Daddy have enough diapers/underwear for _____ *[insert the child's name in the blank].*

Thank You, Jesus, for diapers/clean pants. They make me feel so much better. Amen.

Theme: Clean Clothes

Bath Time

It's bath time! We need to take a bath every day so we can stay fresh and clean and smell good. Water is good for our bodies. It washes off all the dirty spots and helps us feel nice and relaxed. Here is your washcloth.

[Sing to the tune of "Old MacDonald Had a Farm" and substitute the child's name.]

"*Vanessa* likes to take a bath,
  Take a bath each day.

Jesus made the water warm,
Take a bath each day.
With a wash, wash here,
And a wash, wash there,
Here a wash, there a wash,
Everywhere a wash, wash,
Vanessa likes to take a bath,
Take a bath each day."

Thank You, Jesus, for warm water. Amen.

Theme: Keeping Clean

#54

Making a Joyful Noise

Materials: *rattle, squeaky toy, paper, drum*

This is a rattle. It makes a noise when you shake it.

This is a squeaky toy. It makes a noise when you squeeze it.

This is paper. It makes a noise when you crinkle it.

This is a drum. It makes a noise when you hit it.

The Bible says to.

[Sing to the tune of "Row, Row, Row Your Boat."]

"Make, make, make a noise,
  Make a joyful noise.
  Jesus loves to hear our noise,
  Jesus loves our noise."

Can you think of other ways to make a joyful noise?

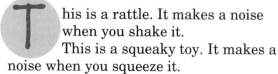

#55

Theme: Being Happy

Nap Time Devotional

Materials: *stuffed animals*

I nsert the child's name instead of *Vanessa*.]
Sometimes it's fun to make noise, but sometimes it's good to be quiet. God wants us to have quiet times and to rest. In the Bible He says, "Be still and know that I am God." Can *Vanessa* be still? Yes! *Vanessa* can be still.

Here are *Vanessa*'s stuffed animals. This is *Vanessa*'s dog. *Vanessa*'s dog runs back and forth, back and forth! He barks,

"Woof, woof, woof, woof."
Be still, little doggy; it's time for quiet time now.

This is *Vanessa*'s kitty. *Vanessa*'s kitty climbs up on her bed. It rubs against her legs. "Meow," says the kitty. "Meow."

Shh, little kitty; it's quiet time now.

[Repeat with no more than two animals per year of the child's age.]

Now it's time for *Vanessa* to be still too. It's time for a rest. Sleep well, *Vanessa*.

Theme: I Need Rest

#56

Devotion

Elephants and Me

Materials: *stuffed elephant or picture of elephant*

Show the child a stuffed elephant or a picture of a live elephant.]
        A baby elephant has big ears. *[Point to ears.] Vanessa* has little ears.
        A baby elephant has a long nose. *Vanessa* has a little nose.
        These things are DIFFERENT.
        But the baby elephant has a mommy who takes care of it. And *Vanessa* has a mommy who takes care of her. That is the SAME. God gave mommies to all babies and very young animals because He knew they would need someone to help take care of them.
        [Repeat with other animals, as the child's attention span allows, stressing things that are different but that having a mommy is the same.]
        Thank You, God, for mommies. Amen.

#57

Theme: I Love Mommy!

Zebras and Me

Materials: *stuffed zebra, picture of baby zebra, or substitute favorite animal*

Fill in the child's name instead of Vanessa.]

Baby zebras have little black noses. *Vanessa* has a little brown nose. *[Fill in skin color as appropriate to the child.]* Our noses are different.

Baby zebras have a little skinny tail. *Vanessa* doesn't have a tail. That is different.

Baby zebras have two ears. *Vanessa* has two ears too—one on each side of her head. That is the same.

Baby zebras have striped skin, black and white. *Vanessa* has smooth, pretty brown skin, all the same color. Our skin is different.

But baby zebras look just like their mommies, and *Vanessa* looks just like her mommy.

Jesus made babies to look like their mommies. A baby zebra always looks like its mommy. A baby lion always looks like its mommy. And a baby girl (or boy) looks like her (his) mommy. That is the same.

That's the way God made babies to be. God is so wise.

Thank You, God, for making me look like my mommy. Amen.

Theme: Nature

#58

Furry Animals

S how the child a picture of a buffalo, or any furry animal, and fill in the animal name as appropriate.]

This is a buffalo, and this is a baby buffalo. A baby buffalo has furry skin that keeps it nice and warm, because it gets very cold sometimes where buffalo live.

You don't have furry skin. That's because you have clothes to wear. And when it's cold, you have a warm blanket to snuggle under.

God knew that the baby buffalo didn't have a warm blanket, so God made one right on its skin!

[Repeat with other animals, if the child's attention span will allow.]

God is so wise. He knows how to make each animal just right.

Thank You, God, for making my skin just right. Amen.

Theme: Nature

The Anteater

Materials: *plastic ants, picture of anteater, jar, yarn, glue*

*U*se a bag of small plastic ants from a nature store or use a hole punch on black construction paper and make many little black spots. Pretend these spots are ants.]

Ants are little bugs that crawl, and almost look like little black dots. This animal *[show picture of an anteater]* eats ants. *[Drop the plastic ants or construction paper spots into a jar.]* Ants live outside, under logs and on top of them, and in the grass and in the dirt. The anteater can't reach them there.

So God gave the anteater a long sticky tongue. *[Dip a length of yarn in glue until it is sticky all the way down, and have the child lower the end into the jar. The pretend ants will stick to it.]* The anteater's tongue is just like this. It can stick its tongue down in a hole and the little ants will stick to it. God made the anteater's tongue so that it could get dinner.

You have a little round pink tongue because God didn't plan for you to eat ants.

Thank You, God, for not designing me to eat ants. Amen.

Theme: Nature

#60

Growing Seeds

Materials: *brown construction paper, sheet of clear acrylic, glue, seeds, flower stickers*

S queeze several dots of glue on the construction paper. Help the child glue a seed to each dot. Then place the clear page over the brown paper. Punch holes in sheets and loop string or a ring through holes, or place in a three-ring notebook.]

Jesus made a special way for us to grow plants. The same thing works whether we are planting flowers or vegetables. We plant the seed in the dirt. Jesus sends the rain to water it, and soon we have flowers! [Place the clear sheet over the seeds and help the child put a flower sticker over each seed.]

We don't know how to make the flowers grow, but Jesus does. And He makes the seeds grow into flowers or into vegetables. Jesus is so smart!

Dear Jesus, thank You for making seeds grow into good things to eat and pretty things to smell. Amen.

#61

Theme: Nature

Spouting Whales

Materials: *clear acrylic sheet, construction paper (blue and contrasting color), white paper*

F*rom the sheet of contrasting construction paper, draw and cut out a whale shape.]* When a whale surfaces to spout in the ocean, it looks like a big shapeless mound. *[Help the child to glue whale onto the blue sheet. Place the clear acrylic page over the blue sheet. Out of white paper, cut out a spout shape. Let the child glue the spout on the clear page so that it appears to be coming out of the whale.]*

Whales breathe air, just as you and I do, but whales don't have a nose. Instead, they breathe through a hole in the top of their head. When the whale comes up to the top of the water, it blows out the bad air. This makes a big spout in the water. *[Take acrylic sheet off blue page.]* The whale is down in the water. It's holding its breath. Now it needs a breath. It's coming up to the top! Are you ready? *[When you say "Blow," have the child put the acrylic sheet back over the whale so you can see it spout. As soon as you say "OK, it's going back down into the water!" have the child take the acrylic page off again.]*

Thank You, God, for making whales able to spout. Amen.

Theme: Nature

HFJ-6

#62

Insects

Materials: *construction paper, glue, paper, pipe cleaners, tape*

From construction paper cut two small ovals and one large oval. Help the child glue ovals together, end to end (in a snowman shape), on paper. Then let the child either draw in six legs or create legs from pipe cleaners and tape them to the bug. Don't forget to have little antennae coming from its head.]

Insects are bugs. They have three parts to their bodies: a head, a thorax (which means their chest), and a big round tummy. They have six legs because they are INSECTS. (Spiders have eight legs.)

Thank You, God, for making bugs so neat. But thank You for giving me only two legs—I would look funny with six. Amen.

Theme: Nature

Bombardier Beetles

Materials: *small bulb syringe (or any type of squirting device)*

*T*his activity is best done outdoors or in the bathtub.]

The bombardier beetle is a bug, but it is a very special kind of bug. Jesus knew that bugs would have many enemies—birds and some small animals who like to eat them. Jesus cares about bugs, too. He made a very special protection for bombardier beetles. When a bombardier beetle gets scared or thinks it might be in danger, it turns its tail toward the danger and *squirt [squirt water on your child],* it aims at the enemy!

The liquid bombardiers squirt tastes bad to other animals and stings their eyes. This gives the beetle time to get away. Now it's your turn to be the bombardier beetle. Do you sense danger? What are you going to do? *[Take turns being the bombardier beetle.]*

Thank You, God, for giving protection to the bombardier beetle, and thank You for giving me an angel to protect me so I don't have to squirt like the beetle. Amen.

Theme: Nature

#64

Zacchaeus

Materials: *heavy paper or light cardboard, marker pen, green fabric, glue*

Cut an uneven green oval from the fabric for a tree shape. Have the child glue only the top edge of the fabric to the cardboard. Use marker pen to draw a trunk. Pull back the fabric and draw a little stick man under the green part of the tree.]

Zacchaeus was a very short man. He heard that Jesus was coming to his town. He wanted to see Jesus so badly! But when Jesus came, there were so many people around him that Zacchaeus couldn't see. He jumped and jumped, but he still could not see over the people. So Zacchaeus climbed up in a big tree. He thought that he'd be able to hide up there and look down and see Jesus, and nobody would know that he was there. *[Lift up fabric to reveal stick man.]* Peek-a-boo! Jesus knew Zacchaeus was in the tree. Zacchaeus thought he was hiding, but peek-a-boo! Jesus could see him.

Sometimes we think we're able to hide too, but we can never hide from Jesus. No matter where we are, peek-a-boo, Jesus sees us and He loves us.

Dear Jesus, thank You for always knowing where I am and for taking care of me. Amen.

Theme: God's Word

The City of Jericho

Materials: *pillows, party noisemakers*

Stack pillows or cushions in the middle of the room to represent Jericho. *Provide the child and yourself with a party noisemaker (the type you blow in).]*

The children of Israel were afraid. Jericho was a big city with tall, thick walls around it. God told them to march around Jericho one time each day for six days. On the seventh day they were to march around the city seven times. The first six times they were to march around it quietly. But the seventh time they were to blow their trumpets and make lots of noise. *[March with the child six times, silently, around pillow pile.]*

"Now remember, on the seventh time, when we get all the way around, we're going to blow our horns and make lots of noise." *[March around Jericho silently the seventh time.]* "Are you ready? Blow!" *[After making a loud noise, allow the child to help you knock "Jericho" down.]*

God is awesome! The children of Israel didn't have to fight the people of Jericho at all. God knocked the city down when they did what He told them to.

Thank You, God. You are so good! Amen.

Theme: God's Word

#66

Follow Me

Assign each child the name of a different disciple, such as Peter, James, John, Andrew, etc. Have them all sit down until you call each one in turn. Walk up to the first child and say, "Jesus said to Andrew, 'Come, follow Me.'" Have the child follow you. Play follow the leader around the room, then approach the next child. "Jesus said to Matthew, 'Come, follow Me,'" etc. Repeat until everyone is following Jesus. Then repeat, allowing each child to have a turn to be Jesus and invite the others to follow.]

Dear Jesus, I want to follow You too. Amen.

Theme: Discipleship

Blue Tassels

Materials: *deep-blue yarn, cardboard, scissors*

W*rap yarn around a four-inch piece of cardboard 20 times. Slide a thread of yarn under the entire loop and tie a knot. Slide the cardboard out of the loop. Hold the yarn loop by the knot and clip yarn at the other end. Now you have a tassel.]*

In Bible times the dye that was used to make blue thread was very expensive. Only kings and royalty were able to afford it. It became the tradition that only they were allowed to wear the color blue. When God helped His people escape from Egypt with Moses, He made several changes in their lives. They had been slaves and had had to do everything they were told by their masters. Now God said, "No matter how poor each family is, they get to wear a little blue tassel on their clothes." Now they weren't slaves anymore! Every single person was royalty. They were part of God's family.

When we join God's family, that makes us royalty, too. You may wear this blue tassel on your shirt to remind you that you are a prince.

Dear Jesus, thank You for letting me be part of Your family. You are a wonderful king. Amen.

Theme: God's Family

#68

Plagues of Egypt

Materials: *small plastic animals, ice cubes*

This activity is best done outside. Place the plastic animals on the ground.]

For a while God's people were slaves in Egypt. They had to work very hard and were treated badly. God sent Moses to rescue them. Moses told Pharaoh, "God says let My people go."

Pharaoh said, "No."

So God told Moses, "I am going to send some terrible plagues on Egypt." One of them was a plague of hail. Sure enough, God did just what He said. Big chunks of ice fell from the sky. *[Drop ice cubes on plastic animals a few at a time. Allow the child to drop several on the animals too.]*

The ice hit all the people and animals that weren't inside for shelter. It was a terrible plague. It hurt many of the Egyptians, and it killed some of their animals. God loved His people. He did not want them to be treated unkindly. That is why He sent the plagues on Egypt.

Thank You, God, for taking such good care of Your people, and thank You for taking care of me, too. Amen.

Theme: God's Word

Blood on the Door

Materials: *red paint, paintbrush, large cardboard box*

[*This activity is best done outside.]*
Let's pretend we are a slave family in Egypt. We work for Pharaoh. He has been very mean to us. We have to work very hard and are not treated nicely. Moses has told us that tonight we will be leaving Egypt. It is so exciting! But we don't know how he is going to work it out. Pharaoh still says we can't go. *[Cut a hole in the cardboard box for a door.]* Pretend this is our house and this is the door.

Moses tells us God's angel of death is going to come through Egypt and kill the oldest child in every home tonight. Only the children in the houses where there is blood on the doorpost will be safe. Should we obey Moses? Yes! Let's obey Moses. *[Help the child paint red paint on both sides of the door and across the top.]* There, now our house has blood on the doorposts on both sides and above it, just like Moses told us to. Now you will be safe tonight when the angel comes over.

God still protects His children, but we don't have to put blood on the door anymore. All we have to do is obey Him.

Theme: God's Word

#70

Thankful Bingo

Materials: *paper, marker pens, stickers, 3" x 5" cards*

For younger preschoolers, divide paper into four sections. More advanced children may divide it into nine, 12, or 16 sections. Allow the child to place a different sticker of objects for which he/she is thankful in each square on the page. Then place an identical sticker on a 3" x 5" card for each sticker on the page. Many sticker packages come with four sheets of stickers, making it convenient to make a set of cards and three different thank-You Bingo pages.

[Mix up the cards. Draw one card at a time, allowing everyone to cover the object on their paper from the card. Use 3" x 5" cards cut in half, pennies, or some other object to cover pictures. The first person to cover their objects wins. Say a thank-You prayer for each object on your sheet.

[Cards may be made on stiffer card stock and laminated with clear vinyl to make them last longer. Children will want to play this again and again.]

Theme: Thankfulness

Turkeys

Materials: *paper, marker pens*

W ild turkeys can fly, but most turkeys on farms are too fat to fly and just run around on the ground. Chickens say "Cluck, cluck, cluck." Roosters say "Cock-a-doodle-doo." Ducks say "Quack, quack, quack." But the turkey says "Gobble, gobble, gobble." *[Have the child place his/her hand, palm down, on the paper. With a marker pen, draw around entire hand, making a straight line across the bottom of palm. Turn the paper so thumb is pointing directly up.]*

This is the turkey's head. *[Have the child put a dot on it for an eye and draw a beak.]*

Turkeys have little things hanging down under their beak called "wattles." *[Draw a teardrop shape under its beak.]*

[Point to the lines around the child's fingers.] These are its tail feathers. Do you want to draw some more? *[Allow the child to draw a few more feathers in between the finger feathers that are already there. Draw legs and three-toed feet.]*

Dear God, You are so wise. Thank You for making turkeys. Amen.

Theme: Nature

#72

Devotion

Missionaries

Materials: *brown construction paper, stapler or Scotch tape, popsicle stick, pipe cleaners*

In North America, telling people about Jesus is pretty easy. You can tell them by talking to them, you can tell them on the phone, you can ride to their house to tell them, or you can fly to the city where they live.

In other countries it's not as easy to get around. People who go to other countries to tell people about Jesus are called missionaries. To get to some countries, they have to go by boat. In other countries they have to take canoes up rivers.

We're going to make a missionary and a canoe. *[Make a pipe cleaner man shape. Carefully fold the brown construction paper canoe in half, but do not crease it. Staple or tape the ends together, leaving the middle part round so you have a canoe shape. Place your pipe cleaner missionary in the canoe, and let him hang on to the popsicle stick oar.]*

Dear God, I want to tell people about You, too, and be a missionary, whether it's here in this country or somewhere else in the world. As I grow, show me who You want me to tell and where I should go. Amen.

Theme: Witnessing

The Waldenses

Materials: *bread dough or package of biscuit dough, Bible verse on piece of paper*

ake sure the Bible verse is not written with water soluble markers or it will smear during baking.]

The Waldenses lived a long time ago. The king didn't want people to be able to read the Bible. So the Waldenses wrote Bible verses on paper and copied them for their friends, but they had to hide them when the king's men came around. One day a woman was making bread when the king's soldiers came. Quickly she folded up the Bible verses and hid them in the bread dough. *[Give the child a piece of dough and a piece of paper with a Bible verse on it. Have the child fold up the verse and fold up dough around it. Bake according to instructions on dough package. Let it cool.]*

When the soldiers went away the woman brought her bread out of the oven, opened it up, and there were her Bible verses, nice and safe! *[Open up the bread and retrieve the child's Bible verse.]*

Dear Jesus, thank You for keeping your Bible safe through all the long years and for helping us to know what to do in emergencies. Amen.

Theme: Faithfulness

#74

The Pilgrims

Material: *cooked corn*

Have the child count out five kernels of corn and place them in a bowl.] When people first came from Europe to settle in America, they went through a very hard winter. They didn't have enough food. Their records tell us that sometimes they got only five kernels of corn apiece for a meal. That isn't very much to eat at all. *[Have the child eat the corn.]* Are you still hungry? Yes, they were too.

God sent them someone who helped them grow more food in their gardens so they would have enough to eat. His name was Squanto. Squanto was a Native American who knew the best way to grow food in America. He loved God. People who love God help others.

The hungry people were so happy, because they were not hungry anymore. I'm so happy God has given us enough food to eat. I would be hungry too if we had only five kernels of corn at a time!

Thank You, God, for this food, and thank You for giving us enough to eat. Amen.

Theme: Thankfulness

Thankfulness

Materials: *popcorn, kidney beans, or marbles, bowl*

G*ive each child five kernels of popcorn, dried kidney beans, or marbles, etc. Pass a bowl around the table to each person in turn. Have them say one thing they are thankful for and drop a* bean in the bowl, then pass it on to the next person until everyone has put all of their beans in the bowl.]

Thank You, God, for each thing we mentioned. Amen.

Theme: Thankfulness

#76

Nerves

Do you know what nerves are? They are little fibers (like little strings or soft wires) inside your skin, all over your body, that make you able to feel. *[Have the child lie on his/her tummy on the floor and give him/her a back rub.]* If you had no nerves inside your skin, you wouldn't be able to feel this back rub or be able to feel anything touching you at all!

Thank You, God, for making nerves in my back so I can feel this nice back rub. Amen.

Theme: Healthy Body

Guess Who Gang

Materials: *3" x 5" cards, bowl*

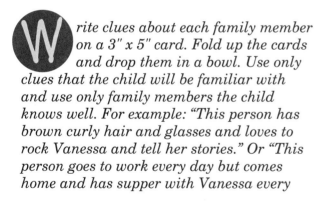

Write clues about each family member on a 3" x 5" card. Fold up the cards and drop them in a bowl. Use only clues that the child will be familiar with and use only family members the child knows well. For example: "This person has brown curly hair and glasses and loves to rock Vanessa and tell her stories." Or "This person goes to work every day but comes home and has supper with Vanessa every night. She loves her very much," etc.

[Make sure to include Jesus. "Vanessa can't see this Person, but He loves her very much. He made everything in her world and gave her a family who loves her and a place to live. She prays to Him every night."

[Your child will want to play this game again and again. As your child gets older, add more people to the clue bowl, and have a prayer and thank God for each person.]

Theme: Love

HFJ-7

#78

Puzzles

Materials: *magazine, glue, scissors, heavy paper*

L et the child select a favorite picture from a magazine. Cut the page out and help the child glue it on heavy paper. Then cut the picture into four pieces (nine pieces for a more advanced child). Mix the pieces up, then help the child fit the pieces together to make the picture.]

Sometimes when we don't understand how things work together, we can ask Jesus. Jesus always understands, and He always helps us figure things out, no matter what the problem is. God is so wise!

Dear God, I'm so glad You always understand how things work. Thank You for being willing to help me. Amen.

Theme: Problem-solving

Rainy Days

oday is a rainy day. We can't go outside to play, but we can pretend it is a sunny day.

[Make sandwiches and drinks and other picnic food. Spread a sheet on the floor in the living room and have a picnic.]*

Thank You, God, that even on rainy days we can pretend it is sunny outside. Amen.

Theme: Being Happy

#80

Mosaic Art

Materials: *coloring book, scissors, bowls, popcorn, dry peas, beans, lentils, rice, glue*

L et the child select a favorite picture from a coloring book. Carefully tear the page out and even the edge with scissors. Provide several small bowls with a variety of dried popcorn, peas, beans, lentils, and rice. Use white glue and accent the lines in the coloring book picture. It will dry clear. While glue is still wet, help the child place the dried grains and beans on the page where the glue is. When it is dry, the picture will be outlined in beans. Do not hang picture up until thoroughly dry.]

Thank You, God, for dried beans and grains. They don't just taste good; they make pretty pictures, too. Amen.

#81

Theme: Good Food

In and Out

Materials: *laundry basket, blanket, teddy bear*

When Moses' mother wanted to hide her baby from the mean pharaoh, she wrapped him in a blanket and put him in a special little basket. *[Wrap your child in a blanket and place him in the laundry basket.]*

Before he was in the basket, he was OUT. *[Lift the child out.]* After she wrapped him up, he was IN. *[Stress IN.]*

God knew where baby Moses was the whole time. God knew where he was when he was IN the basket. *[Lift the child out.]* God knew where Moses was when he was OUT of the basket. God protected Baby Moses when he was IN the basket *[place the child back in the basket]*, and when he was OUT of the basket. *[Repeat, wrapping a teddy bear in a blanket and allowing the child to place the bear in or out appropriately, according to the story.]*

Dear Jesus, thank You for always knowing where I am, whether I am IN or OUT. Amen.

Theme: God's Word

#82

Sea Animals

Materials: *several different sizes of pasta shells and shapes, cardboard, glue*

When we find shells on the beach, we are actually finding the houses of little sea animals. God made soft little sea animals that live in shells. After the sea animal dies, the shell is empty, and the ocean washes it up on the beach. These are what we find when we pick up shells.

God made shells in many pretty colors. He made them in lots of shapes, too.

I have several pretend shells for you. These weren't made by sea animals, but they are the same shape as some of them.

[Allow the child to paint pasta shells in different colors. Use a sheet of cardboard, a small cardboard box, or other papier-mâché shapes that can be purchased in craft stores. Help the child glue the colored shells on the cardboard to make attractive patterns and pictures.]

Thank You, God, for making pretty shells on the beach. Amen.

#83

Theme: Nature

Helpful Insects

Materials: *two wooden spoons, paint, large black pom-poms, and pipe cleaners*

G od made every creature with a special job to do and a way to help the earth. Bees help take pollen from flower to flower. They also make honey. Ladybugs can eat other things on your plants that could hurt them. God made bees and ladybugs to help our gardens.

[Have the preschooler paint the back of one spoon red and the other yellow. Use black to paint a semicircle at the top for the insects' heads, or glue on a black pom-pom. On the bee, paint black horizontal stripes across its spoon body. On the ladybug, paint a thin black line down the middle, then put spots on each side. Use pipe cleaners for antennae.*

[Plant wooden spoon bugs in a planter so that just the bug part is showing in the foliage.]

Thank You, Jesus, for making bugs to help my garden. Amen.

Theme: Nature

#84

Animals With Hooves

Materials: *colored construction paper or felt, Popsicle sticks, glue, scissors*

Cut two fat, wide J shapes from yellow (giraffe), brown (horse), gray (donkey), and white (zebra) construction paper or felt—one set for each animal. To construct each animal, glue a Popsicle stick in the neck area of one J. Cut a one-inch paper or felt fringe and glue it to the outside edge of the J. Cut out appropriately shaped ears for each animal, draw on eyes, spots, and stripes. Plant animal sticks in planters or in a Styrofoam block.]

One family of animals God made on the sixth day have round, hard hooves—horses, donkeys, giraffes, and zebras. People sometimes ride horses and donkeys or use them to carry loads on. But nobody rides on giraffes or zebras. They are wild animals.

The hooves of these animals make it possible for them to run on the ground or across rocks without hurting their feet. God knew what each kind of animal would need, and gave them just the right kind of feet.

Thank You for giving us exactly the feet we need to run and play. Amen.

Theme: Nature

My Family Tree

Materials: *green construction paper, plain circle stickers*

A family tree is a picture of a person's family on a tree. When we pretend our family is a tree, then each person will be a separate branch. We are going to make a picture of our family tree today.

[Give the child a plain, round sticker for each family member. Give the child stickers for any extended family members with whom they are familiar. Draw a smiley face on each circle. Then add hair of the appro-priate color and write the family member's name under each sticker.]

"I'm so glad Jesus made families. Life wouldn't be much fun without a family to live with. And children need grown-ups to take care of them until they are old enough to live by themselves.

Thank You, God, for making my family. [Include names of each family member in prayer.] Amen.

Theme: Family

#86

Inside Fruit

Materials: *construction paper, marker pens, apple, orange, scissors, glue*

S lice vertically through the middle of the fruit. Let the child examine the pattern on the inside. Fold a piece of construction paper in half and cut an apple shape so that part of the apple is on the fold and the apple can open up as a card. Inside the apple, allow the child to glue a white apple shape that's slightly smaller than the original shape and draw on the pattern what he/she sees in the apple. The child may add an optional leaf on the outside. Do the same for an orange, peach, or any other piece of fruit.]

God made fruit for us to eat. He made the skin on the outside to protect it so that bugs wouldn't get in and so that the juice wouldn't leak out. In the very middle of the fruit He put seeds so there would be more fruit.

God knew people would get hungry again and again and want to eat the fruit He made again and again. God created everything so that it could be used but also make more later. God is so smart!

Dear God, thank You for making the fruit for me to eat; and seeds inside so that more fruit can grow for people later. Amen.

Theme: Nature

Day and Night

Materials: *yellow felt, large square of contrasting felt, scissors, glue*

Cut four long, narrow strips from the yellow felt, gluing two vertically and two horizontally, dividing the square into nine smaller squares on the contrasting felt. Cut five moons and five circles for sunshine from the yellow felt.]

God made the daytime and the nighttime. He knew people and animals would need time to sleep. He made people and some animals to play and work and eat in the daytime and to sleep at night. He made other birds and animals to sleep during the daytime and play and work and eat at night. We call these animals "nocturnal."

God made a time for everyone to play, and a time for everyone to rest. It keeps us healthy.

[Teach the child to play tic-tac-toe with the suns and moons on your felt grid. Store in a large Ziploc bag so that the child may play again and again. Each time this game is played, remember to thank God for making the daytime and the nighttime.]

Thank You, God, for making a time for everything and for remembering that all of Your creatures need rest. Amen.

Theme: Healthy Body

#88

Pressing Flowers and Leaves

Materials: *wax paper, flowers and leaves*

Place the flowers and leaves between layers of wax paper and place in book. Replace in the bookcase, where it will be tightly pressed by other books, or stack a heavy weight on top of the book for about a week.]

God made flowers to be pretty and also to grow the seeds for each plant. That way, even after the flowers are gone, more plants can grow, making more flowers. God always made sure that there would be more of everything He created so we would always have enough.

When we pick flowers and place them in water, they look nice for only a day or two. But if we press flowers, they stay nice a very long time. We place them between these papers so that they don't ruin our books. We will check flowers and leaves again after we have waited a week. Then they will be very flat, but they will stay pretty a long, long time, and we can use our pressed flowers to do many things.

Thank You, God, for making flowers, and thank You for making a way for us to keep them longer. Amen.

#89

Theme: Nature

Bookmarkers

Materials: *pressed flowers and leaves, heavy paper, yarn, hole punch, clear contact paper, glue, scissors, paper punch, yarn*

When we are reading a book, often we have to stop before we are to the end. It's nice to have a marker to hold our place. We can make pretty bookmarks out of pressed flowers. These will not only mark our place, but every time we open the book, it will remind us of the pretty flowers and leaves that God made. And we can remember to thank Him for them.

We're going to make a bookmark reminder like that today. *[Cut heavy paper into a 2" x 6" strip. Help the child arrange leaves and flowers as desired and glue them on with white glue. Cover with clear contact paper on both sides and trim the edges. Punch a hole in the end and loop an 8" piece of yarn through the hole. Place in book.]*

Thank You, God, for making flowers. Help me to remember to thank You each time I see my bookmark. Amen.

Theme: Nature

Floral Candle

Materials: *white pillar-type candle, a pot of water deep enough to cover candle, pressed flowers*

T he water we are going to use is very hot, so it's important not to touch the pot or the hot water. I'm going to dip the candle in the hot water by holding the wick. *[Pull the candle out after two or three seconds.]* This makes the wax on the outside of the candle soft. *[Help the child press flowers or leaves into the side of the candle, one piece at a time. Dip in the hot water before each piece is applied to make wax soft enough for the flower to stick. Once material is placed on the candle, dip again and allow to cool three or four minutes to give a wax covering.]*

Sometimes God lets us go through a hard time—like the candle in the hot water. But God always uses it to help us become better. We dip these candles in the hot water to make them soft enough so that we could make them better on the outside. But God uses hard times to help us be better on the inside. See how pretty our candles are? God feels like that when He looks at us after we have gone through hard times.

Dear God, help me to remember that the hard times just make me prettier on the inside. Thank You for Your love. Amen.

#91

Theme: God's Care

Jonah's Shady Place

Materials: *six of the longest dowels available, bean seeds*

Prepare garden soil ahead of time.] After Jonah preached to the people in the city of Nineveh, as God asked him to do, he went to stay on a hill outside of the city. There were some big sticks nearby that looked something like these. *[Point to dowels.]* Jonah sat in the hot sun. Jonah wished he had some shade. God made a vine grow up around all of the sticks and made a shaded place for Jonah. Jonah was so happy.

We are going to make a Jonah tent. *[Stick dowels in the ground in a circle. Pull the tops together and tie them securely.*

Make a circle large enough for the child to sit inside. Plant three or four bean seeds at the foot of each dowel.]

We have planted the seeds, and God will water them with the rain and make them grow. As they grow up the stick, we'll train them so that they cover the sticks and make a tent for you to hide in. Every time you come and sit in your little vine tent you can remember Jonah and how God provided shade for him, too.

Thank You, God, for sending the rain to make my beans grow. Amen.

Theme: God's Word

#92

Spring Flowers

Materials: *pipe cleaners, felt, buttons, chenille wire bees, glue, vase*

Y*ou may wish to cut flower shapes ahead of time. Cut several tulip shapes or five-petal flower shapes from felt. Help child glue flower shapes to the pipe cleaners, then glue a button in the middle. Cut big felt leaves to attach to the stems. Provide a small vase or glass for the child to put flowers in. Add chenille bees if desired.]*

In many parts of the world there is a long cold period called winter. When winter is over, it gets warmer. The plants start to grow. We call it spring. Everyone feels happier when the spring flowers come up. Spring is a happy time. It makes people want to thank God for making it warm and for making everything grow again.

We are going to make some flowers today to remind us that even when it's not springtime, we need to thank God every day.

Thank You, God, for making spring flowers and helping me to remember to thank You all year long—spring, summer, fall, or winter. Amen.

Theme: Nature

Bees

Materials: *yellow and black pipe cleaners, small eyes*

C ut pipe cleaners into four-inch lengths and help the child wrap them tightly around a pencil, alternating black and yellow to make the striped bee-body shape. Pull black into a ball at the end. At the other end, pull the yellow end wire out to make a pointed end to the bee's body.]

God made the bees to help take pollen from flower to flower. They also make honey. Bees have little wings, but when they fly their wings are moving so fast we can hardly see them. When they stop on flowers, often they fold their wings in and you have to look carefully to see them. Bees have little antennae, too, and a stinger on their tail. It's important not to touch bees. When a bee stings someone, it's because it is afraid that person is going to hurt it or hurt its hive. Stinging someone hurts the bee, too. The stinger stays inside the person's skin, and it tears part of the bee's tummy.

We need to appreciate what bees do, but we also need to leave them alone.

Dear God, help me to remember to respect the bees so that I won't get stung. Amen.

Theme: Nature

Caterpillars

Materials: *live caterpillar (or picture), pipe cleaner, eyes, glue*

God made the caterpillars. *[Show the child a picture of a caterpillar if a live one is not available.]* Caterpillars have a special job to do too. Their job is to eat and grow. (This is a lot like your job.) Caterpillars don't stay caterpillars forever, just as babies don't stay babies forever. Babies grow into grown-ups, and caterpillars grow into butterflies.

After a caterpillar has eaten and grown enough, it spins a little cocoon and curls up for a long nap. When it wakes up and the cocoon breaks open, it crawls out. Suddenly it realizes it has wings. The caterpillar is able to stretch its wings and fly because it has become a butterfly. How exciting! We're going to make a caterpillar. *[Use two contrasting colors of pipe cleaner. Help the child wrap the pipe cleaner tightly around a pencil to create a long spring, or caterpillar shape. Tuck the sharp ends in. Glue eyes on. Allow the child to play with it or place it with a potted plant for decoration.]*

Dear God, thank You for making caterpillars that grow into butterflies. And help me to grow up just as You've planned. Amen.

Theme: Nature

Rain Pictures

Materials: *water-soluble marker pens, water color paints, cardboard or fabric*

his is a rainy day. Some people don't like rainy days because they can't play outside. But the rain can be fun. We're going to use the rain today to help us make a pretty picture.

[Use paints or markers to make a picture on this piece of cardboard. When the child has drawn or painted a picture, take it together outdoors and place it in the rain. Wear your raincoats so you can stay out and see what happens. As the raindrops land on the picture, the colors will run together. In a lighter rain you will be able to see where individual raindrops have fallen. You may wish to try rain pictures several times and compare how they look in lighter rains and heavier rains.]

Thank You, God, for making the rain. It helps the flowers to grow, and it makes pretty pictures. Amen.

Theme: Nature

#96

Pond Slime

Materials: *tapioca, construction paper, glue, crayons*

*T*his activity is best done in the spring, when amphibians are laying their eggs. (Or frogs' eggs may be simulated by cooking tapioca.) Using a clear glass jar, scoop up some scummy pond water —the slimier the better—and look for eggs.]

Eggs from frogs and toads look slimy in the water. They look yucky to us. They feel yucky and slimy to our fingers. But God knows each one represents a baby frog or a baby toad. Most frogs' eggs are clumped together in a big lump. Toads' eggs are often in a long, slimy string. [Using dry tapioca, help the child make pictures on construction paper. Glue several tapioca eggs together in a clump next to a picture of a frog, or have the child draw a frog and color it green. On a second sheet of paper, do a long string of tapioca eggs next to a picture of a toad, or have the child draw a toad and color it brown.]

Frogs live in ponds, and toads live on the land, in our gardens.

Thank You, God, for making frogs and toads, and for helping them lay eggs so there will be more frogs and toads. Amen.

#97

Theme: Nature

Time

Material: *a watch with a second hand*

Time can be hard to understand. We know that something that happens soon happens in a short time, and something that takes a long time to happen takes more time.

Let's do an experiment. Crouch down and close your eyes. When you think a minute is up, stand up. I will keep track of the time on my watch and tell you how close you were. *[If you have several children, make this a contest. See who can get closest to one minute.]*

Time seems different to us, depending on what is happening around us. But God always keeps track of time in the same way. And He knows just the right time for each thing to happen. He knows just the right time for a baby to be born, just the right time for us to grow, just the right time for the leaves to come out on the trees, and just the right time for fruit to get ripe.

Thank You, God, that You keep track of just the right time. Amen.

Theme: God's Love

#98

Lydia and Dyed Cloth

Materials: *pair of white shoelaces, marker pens or paint*

I n Bible times, the thread cloth was woven from started out as a white or cream color. Then it had to be dyed whatever color the people wanted it to be. Lydia's job was to dye the thread or the cloth her special color—purple. Purple cloth was very expensive, because the purple dye was expensive.

One day Paul, a friend of Jesus', came to the town where Lydia lived and told her about Jesus. Lydia was so excited she decided to love Jesus, too. She also gave money to Paul so that he could tell more people about Jesus.

We can give money at church so that more people can learn about Jesus, but even more important than that, Jesus wants us to love Him as Lydia did.

[Help the child dye shoelaces by dipping small parts of them in different colors of paint or by coloring on them with markers. When shoelaces are dry, help lace them into the child's shoes.]

Dear Jesus, help me every time I see my pretty shoelaces to remember Lydia. And help me to love You just as Lydia did. Amen.

Theme: God's Word

David's Harp

Materials: *small box, scissors, rubber bands, paint, pencil*

elp the child paint a box. Cut a wide hole in the top. Stretch four rubber bands around the box. Make sure each rubber band crosses the hole. Slide a pencil under the rubber bands on either side of the hole. Place one pencil parallel with the edge of the box. Make the other pencil angled so that the length of each rubber band stretched between the two pencils is different. Allow the child to pluck the rubber bands. Notice that each one makes a different note.]

We don't know exactly what David's harp was like. But we know that he used it to play songs while he watched his sheep. He made up lots of songs to God and sang them to let God know how much he loved Him.

Let's see if we can make up a song, using the notes we can play on our harp, to show God how much we love Him.

[Help the child make up a simple praise song such as "I love Jesus, and He loves me," using the notes on the harp.]

Theme: God's Word

#100

The Shield of Faith

Materials: *cardboard, silver or gold spray paint, duct tape or other strong tape, Exacto knife, glue, optional jewels or decorations*

Ahead of time, cut shield from cardboard, using a newspaper pattern. You can make your shield square, oval, rectangular, or five-sided. Help the child paint it a metallic color to match his/her sword and decorate it with "jewels."]

God gave us invisible armor to protect us from Satan. We can't see the armor, but we can't see Satan either, so it's just perfect. We can read about this armor in the Bible. This big flat piece is called a shield. We can make a handle on the back of it with duct tape and a piece of cardboard. You can hold it up to protect any part of you and stop anything that is thrown at you. Our invisible shield God gave us is called the shield of faith (that means believing that Jesus will take care of us). The problems that Satan throws at us will just bounce off our shield and won't hurt us.

[Have the child practice protecting himself/herself with shield. Roll up several socks and toss them at the child so he/she can bounce them off his/her shield of faith.]

Dear Jesus, thank You for my shield of faith, and thank You for protecting me. Amen.

Theme: God's Protection

Breastplate of Goodness

Materials: *heavy cardboard, silver or gold spray paint, duct tape, Exacto knife, jewels or decorations, glue*

Another piece of invisible armor the Bible tells us about is the breastplate. A breastplate is a chest protector. When we have Jesus in our hearts, He puts His breastplate of His goodness over our chest so Satan can't get into our hearts.

[Cut a piece of cardboard for the breastplate, about the same size as an 8½" x 11" sheet of paper. Help the child paint with metallic paint and decorate. Make shoulder straps from duct tape, placing two strips of tape, sticky sides together. Attach to top of breastplate and to sides at waist so the child can put on the breastplate by sliding his/her arms through straps.]

Thank You, Jesus, for Your breastplate of goodness, which keeps Satan out of my heart. Amen.

Theme: God's Protection

#102

Butterflies and Moths

Materials: *fuzzy pipe cleaners, florist wire, 4" x 6" pieces of felt or tissue paper*

elp the child pleat the felt or tissue paper, then wrap wire around the middle, twisting at the top to form a butterfly or moth. Trim the two pieces of wire to appropriate antenna length.]

God made the moths and butterflies. Some of them are very pretty and brightly colored. Others are brown or other dull colors so that they can hide on tree trunks and in the forest.

Do you know how to tell the difference between a moth and a butterfly? Some people think the brightly colored ones are butterflies, and the dark ones are moths. But this isn't true. Jesus made a special way for us to be able to tell the difference. Look at their antennae. Butterflies have smooth antennae. *[Point to the butterflies made with the florist wire.]* Moths have fuzzy antennae. *[Point to the pipe cleaner antennae on the moth. Look at pictures of butterflies and moths in a nature book encyclopedia and help the child pick out which are butterflies and which are moths by their antennae.]*

Thank You, Jesus, for the beautiful butterflies and moths. Amen.

#103

Theme: Nature

The Gypsy Moth

Materials: *a quarter (coin)*

The gypsy moth is a very tiny moth. It could fit on this coin. *[Show the child a quarter.]* But even though they are so little, Jesus made the gypsy moths very smart. A gypsy moth can find another gypsy moth, even if it is very far away. If you were all alone in this room, and there were people outside, could you find them? What if they were way down the street? What if they were two miles away? Jesus made the gypsy moth able to find another one, even if it's two and a half miles away!

That's a long way. God made them able to do that so that they could find each other and have families, instead of flying around all lost and alone. *[Have the child hide somewhere in the house, then pretend to be a gypsy moth. Fly around, flapping your arms for wings, until you find the child. Then let the child find you.]*

Thank You, God, for always being able to find me. You are even smarter than a gypsy moth. Amen.

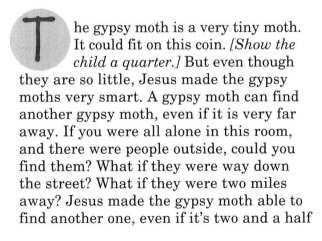

Theme: Nature

#104

Beestings

ave you ever been stung by a bee? It hurts! But did you know that it hurts the bee, too? When a bee stings someone, the bee's stinger remains stuck in the person it stung, pulling it out of the bee's body when the bee flies away. This hurts the inside of the bee's tummy. The bee can't hurt others without hurting itself.

We are a little bit like bees. I don't have a stinger, and neither do you, but it's important for us to remember not to hurt other people, because it can hurt us too.

Sometimes it hurts us right then. When we hit someone, for instance, it can hurt our hand. Or sometimes it hurts us afterward because the person we hurt is very angry with us or because Mom and Dad might punish us for being mean. We need to remember to be like most bees and be careful not to hurt other people.

[Practice being bees. Make a buzzing noise and fly around the room, but be careful not to sting anyone.]

Dear Jesus, help me not to hurt others, because when I do, I also hurt myself. Amen.

#105

Theme: Nature

Bees Wiggle Dance

ees can't talk; they can only buzz. They live together in large family groups in hives or in nests. When one of the bees is out flying and finds a good flower full of nectar, it goes back to tell the other bees so they can all enjoy it. Here's how bees share the good news. They show the bees where to go to find the good nectar by doing a wiggle dance and pointing them in the right direction.

Jesus gave them this way to communicate. I'm glad Jesus made us able to talk. But not all people can talk, and some people can talk but they speak a different language. Try to show me that you're hungry and that you want a drink of water without saying anything out loud. OK. Now I'll show you where to get a drink of water without speaking.

Thank You, Jesus, for making us able to talk. It does make things easier. Amen.

Theme: Nature

#106

Getting Into Heaven

Do you ever wonder who is going to go to heaven to live with Jesus? The Bible tells us that people who have clean hands and a pure heart can live with Jesus. Does that mean that if you get your hands dirty Jesus doesn't love you anymore? Of course not!

When the Bible talks about clean hands and a pure heart, it means hands that don't do bad things and hearts that don't think mean thoughts. What happens if you get your hands dirty? *[Allow the child to answer.]*

Jesus has a way for people who have gotten their hands dirty by doing wrong things to get clean again, too. We can't see the wrong things on our hands, but we can ask Jesus to send His invisible water and wash away the wrong things on our hands. He will make them all clean again, just as our hands get clean when we wash them in the sink when they have mud on them. *[Wash hands in sink with the child.]*

Thank You, Jesus, for giving me clean hands and a pure heart. Amen.

#107

Theme: Having a Pure Heart

Sally's Praying Mantis

Material: *picture of a praying mantis*

Sally was excited. She had found a huge green bug, hanging on to the outside of the screen door. She called her mom to come and look at it.

"Yes," said Mama, "that's a praying mantis. It eats the bad bugs in our garden, so it's a good insect to have around, but don't touch it. They look like they're praying, but they can be mean."

Mama went back in the house, and Sally stayed to watch the mantis. The mantis held its hands up as if they were folded in prayer. It looked like a very good mantis. Sally was sure it wouldn't hurt her. She reached out and petted it softly with her finger. Suddenly the mantis grabbed her finger and bit it hard. Sally cried and ran in the house.

Mama comforted her. "The praying mantis can be mean. It's important when we act like praying Christians not to be mean to other people. Praying Christians should be kind and not be like a praying mantis."

Sally nodded.

Dear Jesus, help me to be a praying Christian and not a praying mantis who hurts other people. Amen.

Theme: Nature

#108

Sally's Closet Door

Materials: *picture of termites and termite damaged wood*

G *o for a walk and find some wood that has been chewed by termites.]*
Sally opened her closet door and took out her shorts and T-shirt, underwear, and socks for that day. She laid them on her bed, then slammed the closet door. As it banged shut, it crumbled and fell into little powdery pieces all over the floor. Sally's closet door had been eaten from the inside by termites. The little bugs had eaten away all the wood on the inside so that all that was left was a little sawdust and powder. Mama swept up the pieces of door with a broom. "Look," she said to Sally. "Here are the termites that got in there and ate your door. It took them a long time. Sometimes when we let bad things into our lives, things we know Jesus wouldn't like, they don't seem to change anything right away, but over a long time they can ruin our whole life, just as the termites ruined your door."

Dear Jesus, please help me not to let anything into my life that would be like these termites. As long as I'm Your friend, I know You'll help me with that. Amen.

Theme: Nature

#109

Lot's Wife

Materials: *piece of dark-colored paper, glue, carton of salt*

O*n the paper, draw a large rectangle with a circle on top to represent Lot's wife as a pillar. Brush the two shapes with glue and have the child sprinkle salt over the picture. Let it dry while you tell the story, then take it outside and shake off the excess salt.]*

Lot and his family lived in a very wicked city. One day two angels came and knocked on the door. They said, "You must come away. Your city is going to be destroyed, and God wants to save you because He loves you and your family. You must come with us—but don't look back."

Lot and his wife and his two girls left the city. They hurried as fast as they could, but Lot's wife didn't want to leave. She turned around and looked back. When she did, she turned into a pillar of salt. God loves us and wants to save us from bad things, but it is important for us to always follow His directions and not be like Lot's wife.

Dear Jesus, help me to remember to follow Your directions. Amen.

Theme: God's Word
HFJ-9

#110

When I'm Afraid

Sometimes I get scared. Everyone has a few things they are afraid of—even your mommy and daddy. Sally was afraid of the dark. Mama used to leave a night-light on in the hall so she wouldn't be afraid at bedtime. She was afraid of snakes, too, and sometimes worried that a snake would get into the house and hide under her bed, even though that never happened.

Are you ever afraid? What kinds of things scare you? The Bible tells us what David did when he was afraid. He wrote, "When I am afraid, I will trust in You."

Whenever we are afraid, we can sing David's song. *[Sing to the tune of "The Wheels on the Bus Go Round and Round."]*

"When I am afraid, I will trust in You,
   trust in You, trust in You.
When I am afraid, I will trust in You,
   trust in You."

Thank You, Jesus, for being close to me so I don't have to be afraid. Amen.

Theme: God's Protection

Round and Round

Show the child a ring, or draw a circle.]
Can you tell where the beginning of this ring is? Can you tell where the end of it is? No. It is all connected. It just goes round and round, on and on. This is like Jesus' love for me. It started before I was ever born, and Jesus will still love me and remember me even if I die before He comes to take us home to heaven.

That's important, because He will wake me up later to be with Him. But Jesus' love for us goes on and on, with no beginning and no end. Jesus loves you that much, too.

[Sing to the tune of "The Wheels on the Bus Go Round and Round."]

"Jesus' love for me goes on and on, on
and on, on and on.
Jesus' love for me goes on and on, on
and on and on."

Dear Jesus, thank You for loving me forever. I love You too! Amen.

Theme: God's Love

#112

My Fingerprints

Materials: *paper, colored ink pad, marker pens*

*P*ress the child's finger onto the ink pad and then make fingerprints or thumbprints on the paper. Notice that pressing harder or softer makes the mark lighter or darker. Also, making a sideways rolling motion can make the print wider. After there are several fingerprints, have the child wash his/her hands.]

You can make your fingerprints into little flowers or animals by drawing legs and ears, faces and whiskers, or stems and petals. Remember, mice have little round ears, rabbits and donkeys have tall skinny ears. And cats have triangular pointed ears.

Look at your fingerprints. On each one we can see little lines going round and round. Your fingerprints are different from anyone else's in the whole world. Each finger has its own special print. By looking at fingerprints experts can tell exactly who made them.

And so can Jesus. Everything about you is unique. There is no one else in the whole world exactly like you. Jesus made you special this way, and He loves you just the way you are.

Thank You, Jesus, for making me unique. Amen.

Theme: I Am Special

Balaam Is Mean to His Donkey

One day a king wanted prophet Balaam to give messages that were not from God. Balaam went with the king's men, even though he knew God did not want him to do this. On the way, his donkey suddenly stopped. "Get going, you silly donkey!" he shouted. But the donkey stopped again. Balaam was even more angry and shouted again. Then the donkey leaned over and squashed Balaam's foot against the wall. Balaam jumped off the donkey and yelled and shouted and took out a stick and started to hit it.

Most donkeys make a braying noise when they are being hurt. *[Have the child make a loud donkey noise.]* But Balaam's donkey actually talked to him. "Why are you hitting me? Haven't I been a good donkey all this time? Haven't I always given you rides where you needed to go?"

Then God let Balaam see that there was an angel in the way with a big sword. Balaam knew he had been wrong to disobey God and wrong to hurt his donkey. Jesus wants us to be kind to our pets, even if they can't talk to us and tell us what they would like.

Theme: God's Word

#114

Balaam's Donkey

Materials: *brown paper grocery sack, brown paper lunch-size sack, blue markers, construction paper or buttons, glue*

Cut two long pointed ears from the large grocery bag. Make them approximately the same length as your small lunch bag The bag opening will be the donkey's neck and the folded bottom of the bag will be its face.

[Help the child glue the ears just under the back side of the bottom of the bag, and the eyes and nose on the flat folded part for the donkey's face. Allow to dry while telling the story. When the glue is dry, have the child place his/her hand inside the bag and tuck his/her fingers into the folded part so that he/she can move the donkey's mouth up and down and make it "talk."]

Now tell the story of Balaam again; this time allow the child to make the donkey talk.

Theme: God's Word

Cat's Whiskers

Materials: *paper plate, construction paper, pipe cleaners, picture of cat*

C*ut triangular ears, round eyes, and nose from construction paper, and glue them on a paper plate to make a cat. Then glue the pipe cleaner whiskers on, making sure they stick out from the plate.]*

Why do you think God gave cats whiskers? [*Look at pictures of cats or at a real cat and observe that the whiskers stick out farther than the cat's head on both sides.*]

God knew that sometimes cats would need to hide. Sometimes they crawl inside a hollow log. Sometimes they crawl into an empty pipe or a box or other hiding place.

Cat's whiskers stick out on each side as far as their body does. When a cat sticks its head in a hole, if its whiskers touch the sides, the cat knows that its body can't fit through the hole, even though its head is small enough. So the cat doesn't get stuck. God is so wise and wonderful, and He cares about all His animals. That's why He made whiskers for the ones who needed them.

Dear Jesus, thank You for giving cats their whiskers and for giving me everything I need. Amen.

Theme: Nature

#116

Hands of All Colors

Materials: *construction paper, color of various skin tones*

Place the child's hand, palm down, on the various colors of construction paper with the fingers stretched out and draw around the hand. Help the child cut out the hands.]

People on our earth have different types of skin. Some people have darker skin, some people have lighter skin. Some people's skin has more of a pink color to it, while others have more of a yellow or a brown, or even a little bit of red. Jesus does not have a favorite skin color. He loves people with brown skin and pink skin, with yellow skin and red skin.

[Sing to the tune of "The Battle Hymn of the Republic" chorus. Vary the words of your song to match the colors of hands that you have cut out.]

"Jesus loves the kids with brown hands;
Jesus loves the kids with pink hands;
Jesus loves the kids with red hands.
Jesus just loves kids."

Thank You for loving and making things of all colors—flowers, animals . . . and people! Amen.

#117

Theme: God's Children

Not a Good Playmate

Materials: *a large rubber ball*

Mike had a new bouncy ball. He played with it every day. One day he left it out in the yard. The next morning, as he was eating breakfast, he looked out the window. There was a little skunk trying to play with his ball. The skunk stood up on its little hind legs and tried to climb on top of the ball. The ball rolled over—and the little skunk did, too. It tried again. It was so funny. Mike and his brother and his mom laughed and laughed.

"Let's go out and play with him," said Mike.

"We can't," said Mama. "A skunk is a wild animal. Skunks can bite, and they also can spray a very bad smell on you if you get too close. Someday, when we go to live with Jesus, the animals won't be afraid of us. But for now we have to watch from the window."

[Play with the rubber ball and have the child pretend to be the little skunk climbing on the ball.]

How glad I am, Jesus, that You are coming soon so that we can live with You and the animals won't be scared anymore. Amen.

Theme: Nature

#118

Pepper and the Snake

Be quiet, Pepper," said Mama. But Pepper kept barking.

"Be quiet, Pepper," said Daddy. But Pepper barked more. "Take Pepper outside," said Daddy.

Sally took Pepper outside, but before she could get back to her place at the table, Pepper had come back in through the doggie door and was barking again.

"There must be something he's upset about," said Mom. "What is he barking at?"

"He's barking at the fridge," said Sally.

Mom and Dad moved the fridge out from the wall and looked behind it. There was a big snake. Jesus made dogs very smart and gave them noses that can smell very well. Pepper could smell the snake behind the fridge and was warning the family.

"I'm so glad Jesus made Pepper that way so he could warn us," said Sally.

[Let the child pretend to be Pepper barking in front of the refrigerator. Then have the child tell you what Pepper would have said if he could talk.]

Thank You, Jesus, for making dogs so smart. Amen.

#119

Theme: Nature

Mr. Bill Calls for Help

Mike was playing in the living room when Mr. Bill flew in and started tweeting at him loudly. *[Have the child flap his/her wings and make birdie noises.]* Mike went back to Mr. Bill's room to see what was wrong. "You have enough food, you have enough water. Everybody looks like they're doing OK," said Mike. "You need to settle down."

Soon Mr. Bill was flapping and squawking for help again. *[Have the child flap and squawk.]* Mike went back to the birdie room and started looking inside the nesting boxes to see if there were new babies. He found Miss Chickie, Mr. Bill's mate, in her nesting box. She was very sick. Mike and his mom took Miss Chickie to the vet. Miss Chickie had an operation and got medicine and was better in just a few days.

Sometimes there are things that we can't do anything to fix, but we can ask a grown-up or another person to help, just as Mr. Bill did.

Dear Jesus, please help me to know when to ask for help, just as Mr. Bill did. Amen.

Theme: Nature

#120

Baby Belladonna Disobeys, Part 1

Materials: *picture of parakeets*

Baby Belladonna was a little blue parakeet. Michael had six pet parakeets who were grown up. They were very good about staying in their part of the room, with their climbing tree and their nesting boxes. But Baby Belladonna hadn't learned this yet. She kept trying to explore. Her mama would squawk and flap at her, as if to say, "Come back; come back!"

Sometimes Baby Belladonna did, but sometimes she kept exploring. Michael would pick her up and say, "No, no, Baby Belladonna. You need to stay in the birdie tree." And he would put her back with the others. But soon she was exploring again. "I am going to have to put you in a birdie cage," said Michael sadly, "because you could get hurt out exploring by yourself."

Was Michael being mean by putting Baby Belladonna in a cage? Are there places your mommy won't let you go? What kind of places are dangerous for people your age to go? Parents make rules to keep us safe. Jesus gives us rules to keep us safe, too.

Thank You, Jesus, for loving us and not wanting us ever to get hurt. Amen.

Theme: Nature

Baby Belladonna Disobeys, Part 2

We are going to play a yes-and-no game. As I tell the story, I will ask you questions. Nod your head if you think the answer is yes, and shake it from side to side if you think it is no.

The next day, when Michael was not looking, Baby Belladonna squeezed herself as tiny as she could and got through the bars of her cage and went exploring again. Was Belladonna being naughty? Yes! Do you think Michael was mad at her? No, but he was worried she would get hurt.

Suddenly Michael heard a loud snap and a squeal. Baby Belladonna had gotten her foot caught in a mousetrap behind the refrigerator. Michael gently picked her up and took her foot out of the trap and comforted her. Poor Baby Belladonna! Her foot wasn't hurt because she was being punished for disobeying, but disobeying took her to a dangerous place, and now she was hurt. Michael was sad, and Belladonna was sad too!

Dear Jesus, please help me not to disobey You or my mom. Amen.

Theme: Nature

#122

Michael Asks Jesus for Help

M ichael was so sad about his baby parakeet and her hurt foot. Baby Belladonna just stood on one leg all the time. "I don't know if it will get better," said the vet, "but we'll just watch her for now."

"Mom," said Mike, "Jesus healed the lame man's leg. Do you think He would heal Baby Belladonna's leg, too?"

"He can," said Mama.

So Michael prayed and asked Jesus to heal Baby Belladonna's leg, but she just stood there on one foot. You have two legs just like Belladonna. Try to get around using only one foot. This is how Baby Belladonna felt.

"Why didn't Jesus heal her?" asked Michael.

"He doesn't always heal people right away, as He did the man in the Bible," said Mama. "Jesus might heal Baby Belladonna's foot, or Jesus might just help Baby Belladonna to get better and get along without her foot. But we can trust Him to take care of her because He loves her."

"Thank You, Jesus, for loving me and Baby Belladonna, even if we do have to wait sometimes," Michael prayed.

#123

Theme: Nature

Jesus Helps Belladonna

Michael was very sad that his baby parakeet, Belladonna, had a paralyzed foot. Michael had made a special home for Belladonna in a large flat tray, where she could have little wood chips to walk on and several little sticks to sit on, since she couldn't climb in the tree that the other parakeets lived in.

For many weeks Belladonna hopped around on one foot. Try to get around the living room on just one foot—remember not to use your hands, because birdies have only wings. How hard it was for little Belladonna!

Then one day after several weeks Michael called, "Mom, come quickly!"

Mom came running. There was Baby Belladonna, perched on the tree, using both feet. Jesus had healed Baby Belladonna. It had just taken some time.

Sometimes Jesus heals quickly, sometimes He heals slowly, and sometimes He just helps us cope with the problem. But whatever it is, He loves us so much.

Thank You for hearing us when we pray, Jesus! Amen.

Theme: Nature

#124

Everyone Has a Job

Michael loved to watch his fish swimming around and playing together. One of his fish was a sucker fish. At least that's what Michael called it. It would suck up to the side of the tank wall, and then use its mouth to suck off all the green algae that had built up. It was Michael's sucker fish that kept the tank walls clean so that Michael could see through the glass and watch his fish.

When Jesus made our world, He gave each animal a job. And Jesus made many kinds of sucker fish, all helping keep their homes clean, whether they live in a fish tank or in a big lake, a river, or an ocean.

We all have jobs to do to keep our world good too. Right now, even though you are little, there are jobs you can do to help. You can pick up your toys. You can help Mom set the table or ask her for another job she would like you to help with. Jesus wants us to all work together to keep our homes a nice place to live, just as Michael's fish all worked together in his fish tank.

Thank You, Jesus, for giving me important work to do to help in my family. Amen.

#125

Theme: Being Responsible

A Job for Mr. Claws

Michael had other things in his fish tank besides fish. In the bottom lived Mr. Claws, a crayfish, or a crawdad. He looked just like a lobster except he was only two inches long. *[Show the child on a ruler how long two inches is.]* Mr. Claws would crawl back and forth on the bottom of the tank. His job was to keep the tank clean too, only he did it by eating the fish poops. This kept the tank nice and clean, but it sounded really disgusting to Michael.

"God made lots of creatures like Mr. Claws that live in the ocean and lakes and rivers," said Mom. "They help keep it clean the same way as Mr. Claws keeps your tank clean."

"By eating 'yuck-yuck' off the bottom?" asked Michael.

"Yes," nodded Mom. "In the Bible Jesus told us not to eat crabs or shellfish."

"If people knew what those kind of animals ate, they wouldn't want to eat them either," said Michael.

Mama laughed. "We can trust the Bible, even when we don't understand."

I'm glad You are so wise, Jesus, and know what is best for us. Amen.

Theme: Nature

HFJ-10

#126

Fresh Food for Fish and Me, Too

Michael took good care of all the creatures in his fish tank. His fish needed things besides the packaged food from the pet store. That worked well when he wasn't able to get them fresh things, but his fish liked fresh food the best. Michael got them different types of pond weeds. His fish loved to nibble on them. Some of his fish liked fresh planarian worms, and he learned how to catch them down by the river. His sucker fish liked an occasional green bean. That made it very happy. His baby turtles liked little minnows. He caught them at the river too. He kept the turtles in a separate tank so they wouldn't eat his other fish.

Just as Michael's fish were healthiest when they ate fresh food, Michael was too. And so are you. Fresh food means things like fruit and vegetables instead of packaged food such as bread and macaroni and cold cereal.

[Share a snack of apple wedges and peanut butter, banana slices, or orange smiles.]

Thank You, Jesus, for giving us fresh food to eat, too. Amen.

Theme: Healthy Body

The Healthy Hero Game

Materials: *magazines and seed catalogs, 3" x 5" cards, towel or pillowcase*

et the child cut out pictures of foods from the magazines and seed catalogs that show healthful fruits and vegetables. Help him / her glue the pictures on 3" x 5" cards. Shuffle the "cards," then show the child each picture, asking if it is a healthful food or not. Make sure you have pictures of desserts, glasses of wine, and other things that the child can identify as not being healthful. When the child has made six correct choices, declare the game won and help him / her put on the healthy hero cape (towel or pillowcase).]

Jesus wants us to be able to make good choices in the things that we eat so that we can be healthy heroes, too. Jesus isn't mad at us when we make bad choices; it just makes Him sad, because He wants us to be the healthiest we can possibly be.

Dear Jesus, help me to always make good choices so that I can be a healthy hero for You. Amen.

Theme: Healthy Body

#128

The Frog in the Closet

Materials: *plastic frog, shoe, container*

One day Michael saw a little frog on a tree. He caught the frog and took it inside. Instead of asking Mom for permission to keep the frog he had found, he decided to hide it in his closet. He put the frog inside his shoe and put a sock over it so it wouldn't hop out.

A few days later Mom was cleaning up in Michael's room. Michael's frog had died inside his shoe and the whole closet smelled bad. Sadly, Michael told her what had happened. "A frog can't live in a shoe in a closet," she said. "Frogs have to live in an aquarium with water and food."

[Have the child place the plastic frog in the container. Add some greenery or green yarn and put a pinch of pretend frog food in.] "If we choose to keep pets inside our houses, God wants us to take good care of them," said Mama. "That's called being a good steward."

Michael nodded. "I will remember that," he said, "and I'm really sorry about the frog."

Dear Jesus, please help me to be a good steward and take good care of my animals. Amen.

#129

Theme: Nature

Sir Isaac Newt

Materials: *damp and dry washcloth, small plastic lizard*

One afternoon Michael was walking with his mom in the woods. "Look at this, Mike," she said, and she turned over a big log. Under the log was a little creature.

"It's a lizard!" cried Michael.

"No, it's a newt," said Mama. "Lizards and newts look a lot alike, but lizards live where it is dry. Newts live where it is damp."

[Have the child feel the damp washcloth, then feel the dry washcloth. Have the child tell you which washcloth a lizard would like, and which one a newt would like.]

"Can I take it home?" asked Michael.

"Yes," said Mama, "but when we fix its house, or habitat, we need to make sure to give it plenty of damp places to hide in, because newts will get sick if they get dry. When God made our world, He made damp places and dry places, because He knew that both lizards and newts would need a home. Michael named his new pet Sir Isaac Newt, and he gave it a damp home to live in.

Thank You, Jesus, for making just the right home for each creature You created. You are so wise. Amen.

Theme: Nature

#130

Conscience and Under- Log Danger

One day Michael turned over a log. Lots of ants scurried back and forth. Some of them carried little white things.

"Those are their babies," said Mama.

"They look really big for babies," said Michael.

"Yes," laughed Mom. "Ants are different than we are."

"Why aren't there any newts under this log?" he asked.

"God put something inside animals to let them know what is safe and what is not. If it is a log that newts are hiding under, it's not a safe place for baby ants to live. And if it's a place where ants are living, it's not a safe place for baby newts to live. We call this instinct."

"Do I have instinct?" asked Michael.

"No," said Mama. "God gave us something even more special. We call it a conscience. When we are about to do something wrong, we have a funny feeling inside that let's us know we shouldn't be doing it."

I'm so glad You gave animals instinct, Jesus, and I'm glad You gave me a conscience. Thank You, Jesus. Amen.

#131

Theme: Nature

Finding Pharaoh's Frogs

Materials: plastic frogs or sheet of frog stickers

Before worship hide frogs in the room, at the child's eye level, in plain sight.]

When Moses lived in Bible times, God's people were slaves in Egypt. They had to work very hard, and Pharaoh, the king of Egypt, was not kind to them. So God sent Moses to ask Pharaoh to let them go. Pharaoh did not want to let God's people leave, because then his people would have to do all the work in Egypt!

God sent several things to help change Pharaoh's mind. One day Pharaoh woke up to find there were frogs *everywhere!* There were frogs in his bed and in his cup. There were frogs in his bath and in his clothes. Pretend you are Pharaoh and try to find all the frogs in this room. How many frogs did you find?

Pharaoh couldn't make frogs. He couldn't even make the frogs go away. God is so powerful. He could make as many frogs as He wanted to because He is the Creator.

Thank You, God, for being strong enough to take care of me all the time. Amen.

Theme: God's Word

#132

Fish Need Water; I Need Air

D onnie was very proud of his two angel fish and wanted to play with them. So he used a cup and, after trying very hard, caught one of them. He carried it over to his bed and poured it out on the bedspread. The fish jumped and flopped. Mama came into the room. "Oh no!" she cried and scooped up the fish and quickly dropped it back in the tank.

"He was upset," explained Mama. "You see, fish breathe water just as you breathe air. Have you ever breathed water?"

"Yes, one time in the bathtub I put my face in the water. I got water up my nose. It burned and made me cough and cough."

"That's how the fish feel when they breathe air," said Mama.

"I'm sorry," Donnie said. "I didn't understand."

"God made just the right things for each of His animals," said Mama. "We need to breathe the air Jesus gave us so that we don't hurt our noses and get sick, and the fish need to breathe water."

"Thank You, Jesus," said Donnie. *"You are so smart."* Amen.

#133

Theme: Nature

God Helps Me Breathe

G od made air for people to breathe. He made water for fish to breathe.

God knew just the right way to make the world so everything He created would have just what they needed. Isn't our God wise! *[Sing to the chorus of "Glory, Glory, Hallelujah!"]*

"God made fish to breathe in water;
God made fish to breathe in water;
God made fish to breathe in water;
But He made the air for me!"

Theme: I Breathe Air!

#134

Abraham Counts the Stars

Materials: *black construction paper, peal-off star stickers*

L*et the child stick as many stars on the paper as he / she wishes.]*
Abraham had no children. He and his wife, Sarah, wanted a baby very badly, but they had never had any. One night Abraham was telling God how much he wanted a child, and God answered him.

"Abraham, someday you will have more children and grandchildren and great-grand-children than there are stars in the sky."

Abraham looked up. He tried to count the stars. He couldn't. There were more stars than he could count. *[Have the child count the stars on the paper. Can he / she count them? If so, have him / her add some more.]*

Abraham had to trust God to keep His promise, and God did! And Abraham did have hundreds of thousands of children, grandchildren, great-grandchildren. God always keeps His promises.

Thank You, Jesus, for always keeping Your word! Amen.

#135

Theme: God's Word

Sally Counts Sand

Material: *small container of sand*

Pour sand onto a plate and ask the child if he/she can count the grains.] Sally had heard how Abraham went to a land that he knew not. She knew God had promised him as many children as there were stars in the sky or grains of sand on the beach. Now Sally and her family were moving to California, a place that she knew not, and she felt just like Abraham.

All of a sudden a police car pulled Dad's car over to the side of the road. Sally rolled down her window and stuck her head out. "Did you know we're just like Abraham? We're going to a place we've never been before. And there's more sand there than we can possibly count, just like in Abraham's story."

"I see," said the police officer. After he talked to Daddy, he talked to Sally again. "That sounds really neat," he said. "You know your stories well. If you can count the sand, write me and tell me about it, OK?"

It makes us happy to share our Bible stories with other people.

Dear Jesus, help me not to be shy about sharing things I've learned about You. Amen.

Theme: Witnessing

#136

Baby Ladybugs

Materials: *stamp pad, paper, marker pens*

*H*elp the child stamp several finger-prints in a circle. Ladybugs come in many different colors. Be creative with your inks. Help the child draw spots on each fingerprint, six little legs, and two antennae.]

Baby ladybugs hatch from little eggs. When the mother ladybug lays the eggs, she covers them with special stuff that the little bugs can smell. When they hatch, they smell the mommy smell on the other babies and try to stay close to them. If they stay all together in a big group, they'll be safer as they grow. By the time the mommy smell wears off they are big enough to make it on their own out in the big world.

Jesus didn't put Christian smell on us, but He wants Christians to stick together in family groups and church groups, because He knows we'll be safer and grow stronger if we stick together with other people who love Jesus and who love us.

Dear Jesus, help me be kind and help-ful and happy so that others will know I love You. Amen.

Theme: Nature

Remember

Materials: *small piece of wood or recycled wooden plaque, several pinch-type clothespins, paint, glue, marker pen, picture of Jesus*

Let the child paint plaque and clothespins. When dry, write "remember" across the plaque with a marker pen. Glue clothespins to plaque. Hang plaque. on wall.]

Have you ever forgotten something important? Some things we forget are not a big problem. Forgetting to play with your favorite teddy bear is not a problem—you could play with it again tomorrow. But forgetting to put your shoes on before you go outside could mean you'll end up with wet, cold feet.

What kinds of things are important to remember? *[Help the child think of two or three things.]* Jesus asked us to remember something important to Him. Jesus wants us to spend one day thinking about Him. We can keep the Sabbath holy by going to church, singing to Jesus, going for walks, and looking at the neat things He's made.

[Hang a picture of Jesus in a clothespin clip.] These clips can hold notes to help Mommy remember things she needs, but we will use one clip to help us remember Jesus.

Thank You for giving me a special day to think about You. I love You! Amen.

Theme: God's Word

#138

Jesus' Boat Story

Materials: *modeling clay or Styrofoam, paper, a straw or pencil*

U se the modeling clay to form a row-boat, or cut one from one-inch thick Styrofoam. Have child stick a pencil in the center of boat. Cut a right-angled paper triangle for the sail. Make a slit near the top and the bottom for the pencil to slip through. Help child mount sail on pencil.]

Jesus and His friends were fishermen. They often went out in their little boat on the Sea of Galilee to catch fish. They would sell the fish the next day so they would have money for the things they needed.

One day the disciples were fishing. They hadn't caught any fish all night long. Jesus called to them, "Try throwing your nets on the other side." The disciples did and caught lots and lots of fish.

Jesus knew right where all the fish were, because He made them and knows all about them. He will help us just as He helped the disciples.

Jesus, it makes me feel safe to know that You will always be there to help me. Amen.

#139

Theme: God's Word

Paul's Boat Story

Materials: *modeling clay, Styrofoam, straws or pencils, construction paper*

Cut a large oval base from Styrofoam, or make it from paper with a ball of clay where each mast should stand. Poke pencil or straw into each ball of clay for mast. Cut two rectangles for the front and back mast and three rectangles for the middle mast. Cut a slit in the top and bottom of each sail, and help the child slide sails onto the pencil.]

Paul had been a preacher for Jesus for a long time. Now he was riding on a big boat, and there were lots of people on it. Paul told the people, "There is going to be a storm, and our boat will crash. But God is going to take care of us, and none of us will drown."

Some of the people were afraid. Some of them believed Paul. The boat tossed and tossed on the waves. *[Have the child rock the boat.]* Then it crashed. *[Pull out the masts and drop them next to the boat.]* Paul and the other people hung on to the masts and pieces of the boat. They all made it safely to an island. God kept everyone safe. God can keep us safe too, even in scary times.

Dear Jesus, thank You for watching over me and keeping me safe. Amen.

Theme: God's Word

#140

Stone Turtles

Materials: *several round, smooth, flat stones, "paint," construction paper or felt scraps*

Have the child paint the stones. Cut out five ovals and a tall skinny triangle from felt or construction paper. Glue to the underside of the turtle so that four feet, a little head, and a tail stick out. Add two dots for eyes.]

Jesus made turtles different than He made you and me or birds or cats. Turtles have a hard shell on their back. This protects their body so that nothing can bite them or hurt them. Jesus knew little turtles would need protection, so He gave them their hard turtle shell.

How does Jesus protect you? *[Suggestions or answers could include: giving me a mom, a dad, a grandma, a guardian angel, etc.]*

Dear Jesus, thank You for loving me and protecting me in other ways so I don't need a hard shell like a turtle. Amen.

Theme: Nature

God Cares About Lizards, Too

Michael was playing in Grandpa's backyard. Suddenly Michael shouted, "Grandpa, there's a dinosaur on your woodpile!"

Grandpa came to look. It did look like a dinosaur, but it wasn't. It was a lizard. "I think this is an iguana," said Grandpa, "although he isn't very green, and it is way too cold for iguanas here." They picked him up and took him into the house in a box. He was very stiff, but his eyes were open.

"Is he OK?" asked Michael.

"Not right now," said Grandpa, "but I think he's going to be. He must have been somebody's pet and got lost accidentally. Poor lizard. He's cold and skinny, and it looks like something bit him on his back. The owners are probably worried about him."

"Maybe that's why God had us find him," suggested Michael. "Isn't it neat that God cares about lizards too?"

"Yes, it is," said Grandpa. "And I'm sure this lizard will be very glad."

"I'm glad too," said Michael.

Thank You, Jesus, for looking after little lizards and for looking after me, too. Amen.

Theme: Nature

Jesus Helps Puff Get Better

Michael named his iguana lizard Puff the Magic Dragon. When he first found Puff, the lizard was cold and skinny and yellow-looking, and had two big sore places on his back. "I think a dog or a raccoon bit him," said Grandpa. "Those sore places look like teeth marks." They washed the bites and put some medicine on them, then they fed Puff some fruit and vegetables. He was very hungry and ate and ate.

Soon he was looking a more healthy green color. The next day when Michael checked on Puff, the lizard was climbing all over his box. He was hungry and ate everything Mike gave him. His bites looked better, too. "I asked God to make Puff better," said Michael. "God helped him overnight."

Grandpa nodded. "Whether God heals somebody right away or takes time to do it, the important thing is that we remember to say thank You."

"Thank You, Jesus," whispered Michael.

Thank You, Jesus, for helping Your creatures when they are hurt. Amen.

#143

Theme: Nature

When Pets Get Scared

Materials: *tape measure, pillow*

Puff the Magic Dragon was a big green iguana lizard who came to live with Michael and his brother, Don. Puff was 30 inches long. *[Use a tape measure to see how long 30 inches is.]*

Even though Puff was a very big lizard, he was very gentle. He liked to sit on Mom's or Dad's shoulder, and though he had sharp claws, he was kind and gentle and never tried to bite. One day Puff was sitting on Don's lap. Don wanted to pick something up from the floor. He leaned over to get it. *[Place a pillow on your child's lap and then have him/her lean over and try to pick something up from the floor.]*

What happened to your pillow? Puff got squashed, too, just as your pillow did when you bent over, and he jumped up and bit Don on the face. Don's face bled, and it hurt. But Don said, "I'm sorry, Puff; I forgot you were there." Don knew that even kind animals can get scared and bite.

Always be kind to animals and not squeeze them or make them feel in danger.

Dear Jesus, help me to be kind to animals and never make them afraid. Amen.

Theme: Nature

#144

Wamml's Temptation

Wamml was a pretty gray parrot with a red tail who lived with Mike and Don. When Puff came to live with Mike and Don, Wamml was curious about him, too. Puff liked to sleep on top of the bookcase in the living room. His long tail hung down in front of the bookcase. Wamml liked to play in his special climbing tree near Puff's bookcase. Wamml would look at Puff's tail hanging down. Sometimes he would lean way out of his tree toward Puff's tail.

"No, no," said Mom. "Don't bite Puff's tail."

"Ooh," said Wamml, and he would be good for a little while. Soon he was leaning toward Puff's tail again. One afternoon there was a great flapping of wings and squawking. Wamml had leaned out too far, trying to nibble Puff's tail, and had fallen out of his tree. Mom picked Wamml up and put him back in his tree. He was not happy.

"When you are tempted to do something wrong, just say no. That's what I do," said Michael.

Jesus, I want to always say no to temptation. I know that makes You happy. Amen.

Theme: Nature

Shake It Off

Paul was a friend of God's. One time when Paul was on a trip on a big ship, there was a wreck. Paul and all his friends made it safely to an island. There, they built a fire to get warm. As they piled more sticks onto the fire, a snake slithered out of the sticks. It was too hot for the snake. It crawled right up a stick, onto Paul's hand, and bit him.

Everybody was scared. Most people who were bitten by that kind of snake died quickly. But Paul knew that Jesus was giving him special protection on this trip, so he just shook the snake off his hand.

Sometimes we get hurt, even when we are doing what Jesus wants us to do too. But most of the time we can trust Jesus and shake it off. *[Have the child practice shaking one hand, and then the other, one foot, and then the other.]* Next time you stub your toe, what are you going to do? *[Practice shaking it off.]*

Dear Jesus, help me be just like Paul and shake my troubles off. Amen.

Theme: God's Word

#146

Shaking My Troubles Off

Paul was bitten by a mean snake while he was on a trip for Jesus. But he just shook it off. When I am doing what Jesus wants me to do, I can learn to shake my troubles off, too. *[Sing to the tune of "Old MacDonald Had a Farm."]*

"When I get hurt, I'll be like Paul;
I'll just shake it off.

God will help me be like Paul;
Help me shake it off.

"With a shake, shake here,
And a shake, shake there.
Here a shake,
There a shake,
Everywhere a shake, shake.
God will help me be like Paul,
Help me shake it off."

#147

Theme: God's Word

Miriam's Tambourine

Materials: *paper plates, beans or macaroni, marker pens, curling ribbon, pipe cleaners, feathers, jingle bells*

After God opened the Red Sea so Moses, Miriam, and Aaron, as well as all of their friends and relatives, could walk across, God closed the sea up behind them so that the Egyptians couldn't hurt them. Everyone was so happy! They wanted to sing a song of praise to God. Miriam was their song leader.

The Bible tells us she led them in singing praise songs to God with her tambourine. *[Lay a paper plate, faceup, on the table. Let the child drop a handful of dried beans or macaroni into it, then place another paper plate facedown on top of the first plate. Have an adult staple the edges all the way around. Decorate with markers. Staple curling ribbon or pipe cleaners to the edges and then curl ribbon or attach jingle bells or other decorations.]*

Now you can sing praise songs to God, too, and, just as Miriam did, tap your tambourine to the music.

Dear Jesus, it's fun to tell You I love You by making music! Amen.

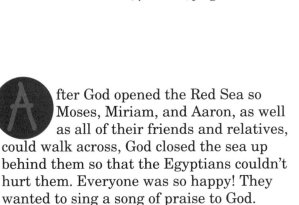

Theme: God's Word

#148

Star Mobile

Materials: *coat hanger, string or yarn, drinking straws, cardboard, felt or art foam*

Cut out star shapes for the child. Optional pizzazz: Let the child paint star shapes with white glue, then sprinkle with glitter. When dry, poke a hole in each star and attach string. Thread string through drinking straws and attach to coat hanger. Hang entire mobile in child's room.]

God created our world, but He didn't create just our world. He created thousands and thousands of other planets and suns. We are so far away that we can't see them from our world, but the suns are so bright that we can see some of them. They look like little pinpoints of light in the sky. We call them stars.

God made so many things we don't even know about. Someday, after Jesus takes us to live in heaven, we'll find out about all kinds of other wonderful things Jesus made all through the universe, but for now we'll have to wait and just look at the stars and think about how awesome God is.

Dear Jesus, I can hardly wait to see all the wonderful planets and suns You've created. Amen.

#149

Theme: God's Word

Elijah and the Ravens

Materials: *construction paper, white crayon marker, or white-colored gel pen*

Help the child cut out several large hearts from black construction paper, an equal number of small hearts from contrasting yellow paper, and two small star shapes for each heart. Turn the black heart upside down, and glue the yellow heart in the middle for a beak. Use a gel pen or white crayon to draw two eyes above beak, and draw lines on wings at the base of the black heart. Glue stars beneath the base for feet. Ravens can be used just like this or taped to a pencil for easier "flying."]

The queen was very angry with prophet Elijah. God told him to hide by a little brook, where he would have water to drink. Every day the ravens flew in to visit Elijah, and every day they brought him some food in their beaks. God never forgot Elijah, and he always had enough food and enough water. God loves you, too, and He will make sure you have everything you need. These ravens will remind you that God will always take care of everything you need.

Thank You, Jesus, for taking such good care of Elijah and me. Amen.

Theme: God's Word

#150

Busy Bees

Materials: *honey, teaspoon*

Honeybees are very hard workers. They have to move their wings very fast in order to fly and make their buzzing noise, much faster than we could flap our arms. They carry pollen from one plant to another, helping them grow. And they make honey.

The bee is very tiny, and even though it works very hard, each bee makes only a little bit of honey. *[Measure out a quarter teaspoon of honey.]* This doesn't seem like very much honey, but it takes three bees their whole lives to make just this much!

Even though each bee is very small, they work very hard and do just what God wants them to do. And even though you are little, you can work hard and do the things God wants you to do, too. Nobody is too little to do what God wants them to, not even bees.

Thank You, Jesus, for being willing to use even little people like me. Amen.

#151

Theme: Nature

Treasure Box

Materials: *empty check box, tissue paper, white glue, glitter, stickers, gummed stars*

Cover one surface of the check box with white glue. Have the child tear colored tissue paper into small pieces less than one-inch square. Glue pieces onto the box, overlapping to completely cover each of the box's outside surfaces. Then embellish with glitter, stickers, or gummed stars. Allow box to dry. White glue will dry clear, so don't worry about places where glue seems thick.]

We've made a treasure box to keep things in that are special to you. We have another treasure box in our house, even though it's not as colorful as your treasure box. It's the Bible. We don't keep things in it, but there are treasures in there just the same. The Bible is full of special promises and encouraging messages from Jesus that help us know how to live. It can cheer us up when we are afraid or discouraged.

Thank You, God, for giving us the special treasures in Your Bible. Amen.

Theme: God's Word

#152

Adam's Friends

Materials: *bottle-sized corks, pencils, white glue, felt or construction paper, marker pens, plastic eyes, pipe cleaner*

Poke a hole in the side of a cork and widen slightly with a sharp knife. Have the child fill the hole with glue and force eraser end of a pencil into the hole. Cut ears from felt or construction paper and have the child glue ears and eyes onto the cork. Small round ears work for bears, triangular ears for cats, and round ears with a skinny sunshine-shaped felt mane for lions. Fringed manes work for horses, giraffes, and zebras; very large ears and a long piece of paper or a pipe cleaner work for an elephant. Use marker pens to color the cork animal face.]

God created lots of animals on our earth to be Adam's friends. Take your animals and plant the pencil end in planters around the room or in a small vase or cup. [Let the child pretend to be Adam, looking around his new garden home, finding each animal and giving it a name.]

Thank You, God, for making all the animals. Amen.

Theme: Nature

Adam's Bird Buddies

Materials: *pencils, bottle-sized corks, glue, construction paper, plastic eyes, feathers*

Poke a hole in the side of the cork and widen with a sharp knife. Let the child fill the hole with glue and place a pencil in the hole. Cut a bill of each shape—long and pointed, short, wide, curved, rounded, and triangular from construction paper, then cut a half-circle for each bird body. Let the child glue eyes and beaks on the corks. Cut out wing shapes and attach, straight side closest to the head, with Scotch tape. By holding the end of the pencil, the child can make the birds fly.]

When God created Adam, He also created lots of bird friends for him. [Ask the child to point to each beak type as you describe it.] Some birds had long skinny beaks for reaching into flowers. Some had round bills for scooping up food from the bottom of a pond. Some had sharp, curved beaks for cracking hard nuts. God knew what type of beak each bird needed. God knew exactly what you would need, too, and He made your body just perfect. [Pretend to be Adam and have the child make the birds fly over to you.]

Dear God, thank You for making all the birds. You are so wise and wonderful! Amen.

Theme: Nature

#154

A Job for Bark

Materials: *paper, large crayons*

Take the child for a walk outside. *Look at several trees; have the child feel the bark.]* On the outside, what does it feel like? *[Place paper over the bark and rub with a crayon to create texture rubbing. Try several different trees.]*

What do you think bark is for? *[After your walk, discuss.]* God gave the trees protection. The inside of a tree trunk has beautiful, smooth wood. God protected it on the outside with bark. The bark protects it from bugs and animals that would like to eat or damage the tree, as well as keeping the inside of the tree safe from the weather. The tree wears its bark like you wear a jacket, except a tree can't take its bark off and on—it wears it all the time.

Thank You, God, for giving bark to protect trees. Amen.

#155

Theme: Nature

Another Job for Bark

Materials: *cinnamon sticks, apple juice*

G od made bark to protect trees, but there are other jobs for bark too. *[Show the child a cinnamon stick.]* This is called a cinnamon stick, but if you look carefully, you'll see it's actually a smooth piece of bark that has been peeled off the tree and rolled up. Only the bark from a certain kind of tree makes cinnamon sticks.

God made each tree different, but this type of bark is good for something else. *[Smell the cinnamon sticks.]* What does that smell like to you? It is cinnamon! We use it in cooking to make things taste good. *[Let the child taste a warm cup of apple juice. Then stir the juice for one minute with the cinnamon stick and let the child taste again.]* Is it different?

God made the bark of the cinnamon tree. It is able to do two jobs—protect the tree and make our food and our apple juice taste good.

Thank You, God! You make such wonderful things. Amen.

Theme: Nature

#156

Angel Helpers

Materials: *paper, pencil, paint, yarn, glitter*

Draw a large triangle on the paper and top with a circle. Have the child draw a nose and mouth on the circle for the angel's face. Pour acrylic or tempera paint mixture into a paper plate. Have the child dip his/her hands, palms down, in the paint. Then place the child's hands on each side of the triangle, making angel wings. Help the child wash his/her hands, then embellish the wings with yarn hair and glitter.]

The Bible says that God knows we need extra help sometimes, so He sends angels to watch over us. The Bible says the angels camp all around us—they are always there, whenever we need them. God loves us so much!

Thank You, God, for sending the angels. Amen.

#157

Theme: God's Care

Counting Fingers

Materials: *construction paper, scissors, marker pens*

Have the child place his / her hands, palms down, on construction paper and draw around each hand with a marker pen. Then help the child cut hands out and glue them to a large sheet of contrasting paper. Using a marker pen, write the numbers 1 to 10, one number on each finger.]

God gave us five fingers on each hand. This means we have 10 fingers we can use to do the things we want to do. God gave us 10 fingers because He knew we could do more things with 10 fingers than if we had only two or three. [Point to each number as you help the child count fingers. This may be an activity you wish to repeat frequently if the child is still learning to count.]

Thank You, God, for giving me 10 fingers. I can do so much more with 10 fingers, but then You knew that. You are awesome! Amen.

Theme: Healthy Body
HFJ-12

#158

Helping-hand Garland

Materials: *paper, pencil, scissors, Scotch tape*

*P*leat a long piece of paper with the pleats no more than three inches wide. Have the child place his/her hand, palm down, on the paper, the thumb touching one side of the pleat and the little finger the other side. Draw around the child's hand and help cut it out. Allow the child to open up the hand garland. You may want to make several and attach them with Scotch tape.]

Jesus made your hands with 10 fingers, five fingers on each hand, so that you can do all kinds of things. We make Jesus happy when we do good things, such as helping Mom pick up our toys. It makes Jesus sad when we use our hands for things that can get us into trouble—taking something that isn't ours, doing things that could hurt us or that hurts someone else. Jesus wants us to use the hands He gave us for good things. *[Place the hand garland up in the child's room to help him/her remember to do only good things with his/her hands.]*

Dear Jesus, please help me to use these wonderful hands You gave me for good things. Amen.

#159

Theme: Healthy Body

Snowflakes

Materials: *Popsicle sticks, unbuttered popcorn, glue, pipe cleaners or paper clips*

When God made our world, He knew it would need wetness. Sometimes God sends the wetness mixed with air. We call this fog. Sometimes it falls in drops of water. We call this rain. And sometimes it gets so cold that the drops of water freeze. These are snowflakes. Some places never get cold enough for the drops of water to freeze. Those places never get snow. *[Help the child glue three Popsicle sticks, intersecting in the middle, to make a snowflake shape. Allow the child to glue popped popcorn along each stick.]*

Your snowflakes aren't exactly the same, and neither are God's. Snowflakes are tiny when they fall from the sky, but if we could look at them very closely, we would notice that each one is perfect, but each one is a little different from every other snowflake. God has so many ways to make snowflakes, just as He made many kinds of animals and birds and fish. *[Hang snowflakes up with pipe cleaners or bent paper clips to remind everyone how wonderful God is.]*

Dear God, thank You for making snowflakes. You are so smart. Amen.

Theme: Nature

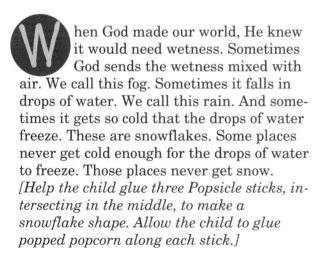

Helping Mom Dust

Materials: *pair of fuzzy socks or old mittens*

Put the socks on the child's hands, pulling them as far up his / her arms as necessary. Show the child which surfaces need dusting, then let him / her help dust. Sing to the tune of "Do You Know the Muffin Man?"]

"I can help my mom to dust,
My mom to dust,
My mom to dust.
I can help my mom to dust;
I help my mommy dust."

It makes Jesus happy when we help Mom. It makes me happy too.

#161

Theme: Helpfulness

Helping Mom Unwrap

T his is a good helping devotion for shopping day. Assign any unwrapping of purchased items such as soap, toilet paper, paper towels. Sing to the tune of "Do You Know the Muffin Man?"]

"I can help my mom unwrap,

My mom unwrap,
My mom unwrap.
I can help my mom unwrap;
I help my mom unwrap."

Thank You, Jesus, for important work to do! Amen.

Theme: Helpfulness

#162

The Story of Queen Esther

Materials: *poster board, marker pens, Exacto knife, pencil, foil*

*U*sing an Exacto knife, cut an oval out of the top half of the poster board, about the right size for the child's face. Cut two armholes in the lower half. Provide markers and help the child draw on hair, a crown, and a beautiful dress for Queen Esther or a beautiful robe for the king.]

One day a mean man tricked the king into making a law that all God's people would be killed. Queen Esther wanted to help, but if she went to see the king, and he did not hold out his gold scepter, she would be killed. [Make a scepter by wrapping foil around a pencil or other object.] Queen Esther prayed and asked God to help her be brave, then she went to see the king. [If the child is a queen, have her place her face and arms through the costume and approach you. Hold out the scepter for her to touch. If the child is a king, have him hold out the scepter as you pretend to be Queen Esther.]

God helped Queen Esther to be brave, and all His people were saved.

Thank You, God, for helping Queen Esther be brave, and help me to be brave when it is important too. Amen.

#163

Theme: God's Word

Pigs Work, Too

Materials: *Scotch tape, bottle, construction paper, pipe cleaner, wooden spoon or pencil, paint*

W hen God created this world, He gave every plant and every animal and every bird a job. Everything was to help all the other living creatures. The pigs had a job, too. Their job was to help clean up. Pigs eat garbage and rotten things so that our world will be nice and tidy and clean. Even though pigs don't smell good, and we certainly wouldn't want to eat one, I'm glad God made pigs, aren't you?

[Help the child paint the bottle with pink paint. Use construction paper or paint for eyes and nostrils on the snout. (Make sure the cap is on the bottle.) Wrap pipe cleaner around a wooden spoon or pencil to make a curly tail and attach it to the flat end of the bottle with Scotch tape. Use construction paper for ears.]

Thank You, Jesus, for making every creature special. Amen.

Theme: Nature

#164

Pinecone Potpourri

Materials: *pinecones, plastic bag, fragrant essential oil*

*C*ollect pinecones with the child. *Place six pinecones in a Ziploc plastic bag. Let the child hold the bag open as you drop six drops of oil fragrance on each pinecone. Seal the bag and ask the child to shake it well. Then dump the pinecones into a bowl or basket.]*

Don't these pinecones smell good now?

God loves things that smell good, too. In Old Testament times, God's people burned special offerings to Him that made a nice smell. God gave us a sense of smell inside our noses. If you hold your nose, you can't smell the pinecones.

Thank You, God, for the pinecones and the oils, and thank You especially for my sense of smell. Amen.

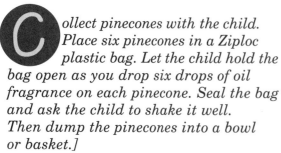

Theme: Healthy Body

Weather Reporter

Materials: *3" x 5" cards, marker pens, magnetic clip or clothespin*

Our world has all different kinds of weather. Some days it is bright and sunny. Some days it is wet and rainy. Sometimes there are loud thunderstorms. In some places there is snow. Sometimes it is warm, and sometimes it is cool.

What is it like outside right now? *[Have the child go outside, then report back about the weather. Help the child draw weather conditions on the 3" x 5" cards. Include clouds, rain, sun, and snow, as appropriate. Include a card for warm, illustrated by a big fire; cold, illustrated by an ice cube, snowman, or a child wearing a sweater. Each day select two cards to report the weather: one indicating either sun, clouds, rain, or snow; the other indicating whether it is warm or cold.]*

God gives us the weather we need. The rain helps the plants to grow. He sends warm sunshine, too. We don't need to be afraid of thunderstorms, because Jesus is with us and provides all the weather.

Thank You, Jesus, for giving us lots of different kinds of weather. Amen.

Theme: Nature

#166

David Sings Praises

When David was a little boy, his job was to take care of the sheep. Sometimes this was hard work. Other times he just had to sit and watch the sheep and keep them company. During these times David made up songs to sing to God. This made God happy. It made David happy, too.

It makes God happy when you sing to Him, too. *[Sing to the chorus of the song "Glory, Glory, Hallelujah!"]*

"I sing praises just like David;
I sing praises just like David;
I sing praises just like David;
I sing my praise to God."

It's fun to tell You I love You by singing! Amen.

#167

Theme: Praising God

Silas Sings Praises

Silas was God's friend. He was Paul's friend, too. One time Paul and Silas took a trip together to tell people about Jesus. On their trip some mean men beat them up and threw them in jail. Nobody is ever very happy to be in jail, but Silas and his friend, Paul, sang songs to Jesus anyway. They didn't sing because they liked jail, they sang because they loved God.

Even when things happen that I don't like, I can still sing to God. *[Sing to the chorus of "Glory, Glory, Hallelujah!"]*

"I sing praises, just like Silas!
I sing praises, just like Silas!
I sing praises, just like Silas!
I sing my praise to God."

Dear Jesus, I can always sing to You, even when things happen that I don't like. Amen.

Theme: Praising God

#168

Hezekiah's Clock

Materials: *clock, or watch, with second hand; paper plate, construction paper, brass fastener*

otice that the second hand always goes around in the same direction. If you watched the clock long enough, you'd notice that the other hands on the clock go around in the same direction as this hand, only slower. *[Mark numbers on paper plate, and help child fasten construction paper hands to clock face with brass fastener.]* Which direction should the hands on your clock go around?

Hezekiah was a king. He was very sick. He called God's prophet to ask him if God would help him get well. The prophet said

Yes. "How do I know it is really God?" asked Hezekiah.

The prophet told him that his clock would go backward that afternoon. Do you think his clock really went backward? Yes, it did! Wise men came from far away places to ask about the God who could make clocks go backward. *[Have child make his paper clock go backwards too.]* Our God is so wise that He can do much more than make clocks go backward.

Thank You, Jesus, for being so wise and wonderful! Amen.

Theme: God's Word

God's Special Candlesticks

Materials: *plastic straws, construction paper, scissors, Scotch tape*

Moses loved God. Moses helped build the first temple to God on our earth. In it was a special candlestick that could hold seven lights. God gave Moses the exact instructions so the candlestick would be just like the one He had in heaven. We don't know exactly what it looked like, but we will make one with seven lights, too.

[Fold a sheet of construction paper in fourths. Tuck ends together to make a triangular tent. Cut seven small slits in the top ridge of the tent. "Pole" the straws up through the holes so that their bases stand inside the tent. Use Scotch tape to help give them stability. Cut tiny "flames" from orange construction paper and help the child tape them to the tops of the candles.]

These flames never went out, reminding the people that God was always with them and would never leave them. Our candlesticks can remind us of that too. Isn't God good?

Thank You for promising to be with me always. I love You! Amen.

Theme: God's Word

#170

God Loves Me All the Time

God loves us all the time. He loves us when we are good. He knows that loving Him will keep us safe and happy. God loves us when we have been naughty, too. It makes Him sad, though, because He knows that when we disobey, we can get in trouble and, sometimes, we can get hurt. But He never stops loving us.

[Sing to the tune of "The Farmer in the Dell."]

"God loves me when I'm good;
 He loves me when I'm good.
 It makes Him happy
 When I do the things I should.

"He loves me when I'm bad;
 He loves me when I'm bad.
 Though it makes Him very sad,
 He loves me when I'm bad."

Thank You, Jesus, for loving me, no matter what. Amen.

#171

Theme: God's Love

Yes/No Golden Rule Quiz

When Jesus was here on earth, most people liked Him—but not everyone. Even though He was very good and kind and helped lots of people, some people hated Him. One day these bad people got together and captured Jesus. They hit Him and spit on Him. It was very sad. Jesus did not like being treated this way. I wouldn't, either!

Jesus wants us to treat others as we would want them to treat us. Answer yes or no to these questions:

Are we pleasing Jesus when we share with our friends?

Do we please Him when we spit on them? Is Jesus happy when we hit our friends? Is He happy when we are kind to them? Jesus doesn't live here on earth anymore, but we can show Him how much we love Him by being kind to our friends and treating them the way we would treat Jesus if He were here.

Dear Jesus, I want to show You how much I love You by being kind to others. Amen.

Theme: Being Kind

#172

Jesus' Faithful Friends

When Jesus lived here on earth, He had many friends. When the mean people hurt Jesus, many of His friends ran away because they were afraid. Even some of His most special disciples were afraid and pretended they didn't know Jesus. Some of His friends were faithful, though, and stayed near Him so He wouldn't be alone. One of these friends was Mary. Another friend was John.

I want to be one of Jesus' faithful friends, no matter what. And Jesus has promised to be a faithful friend to me, too!

[Sing to the chorus of "Glory, Glory, Halelluja."]

"I am faithful, just like Mary;
I am faithful, just like Mary;
I am faithful, just like Mary;
'Cause I am Jesus' friend."

[Alternate words: "I am faithful, just like John was . . ."]
Dear Jesus, I want to always be Your faithful friend. I love You. Amen.

Theme: Being Jesus' Friend

Sin Problems

Material: *chocolate pudding*

S *pread chocolate pudding on clean smooth surface.]*
    Every morning Jesus gives us a brand new day in which to love Him. It is totally perfect, just like this smooth pudding. When we do things that make Jesus sad, it makes marks in our day. *[Use your finger to pock the smooth pudding surface. Allow the child to add extra pockmarks.]*

It makes us feel sad when our day is ruined. Jesus doesn't want us to be sad,

though. He wants us to come to Him and ask Him for help. Then He fixes our day *[smooth pudding over]* as if our mistakes had never happened. Isn't Jesus good?

[Discuss the types of things that might mar the child's day and allow him/her to add marks to the pudding. Practice asking Jesus to fix it and smoothing it over. When finished, lick fingers!]

Jesus, thank You for fixing my day and forgetting my mistakes. Amen.

Theme: Prayer

HFJ-13

#174

Eve's Choice

Materials: *panty hose or tights, marker pens, plastic eyes, glue*

Cut one leg from an old pair of panty hose or tights. Pull it onto your arm to make a snake puppet. Help the child decorate the "snake" with water-soluble markers, adding eyes and markings.]

Adam and Eve, the first people, lived in a garden home that was perfect. God had given them only one rule: Don't touch the tree in the middle of the garden!

One day Eve was looking at the tree. Suddenly she heard a voice! *[Emphasizing the S sounds will make the snake sound "snakey." But remember, the goal is to* teach the story, not scare the child.] What answer should Eve give the snake? *[Allow time after each snake question for the child to answer.]*

Snake Puppet: Say, wouldn't you like some fruit from this tree? You don't think anything bad would really happen if you ate this, do you? Don't you think it would be OK to try it just this once?

If Eve had answered no, she would have been able to live in her garden home forever.

Dear Jesus, help me always obey Your rules so I will be happy. Amen.

#175

Theme: God's Word

Jesus' Wedding

Materials: *formal dress-up clothes, lace or pillowcase for bridal veil, flowers for boutonniere or bouquet*

T*his activity will be enjoyed by children who like playing dress-up and/or who have attended a wedding.]*

When a grown-up man and woman love each other, they don't like being apart. If they decide they want to be together forever, they get married. This means they will have a ceremony and promise God they will love each other. Then they can live in the same place and be together all the time. *[If appropriate, show the child the parents' wedding pictures, or use other pictures of a wedding.]*

Jesus wants to marry us. It's not exactly the same as a human wedding because He isn't just a man; He is our God, too. He talks about this in the Bible, where He calls the church His bride. I'm looking forward to our wedding with Jesus. He has already promised to always love us. When the wedding takes place, then we can go home and live with Him. Do you want to be part of Jesus' bride? He already loves you. You just need to love Him back. I can't wait until it is time for this wedding!

Dear Jesus, I can't wait until You come to take us to live with You! Amen.

Theme: Jesus Is Coming!

#176

Jesus Comes Again, Part 1

The Bible says that Jesus is coming back to our earth again. But this time He won't come as a baby—He will come as the king of the universe! Everyone in the world will see Jesus come. All Jesus' friends will be so happy to see Him.

People like you and me will be excited to see Him.

People who have been dead a long time will be excited to see Him. God will wake them up so they can see Jesus coming, too.

[Sing to the tune of "The Farmer in the Dell."]

"Now Jesus is our king;
Now Jesus is our king;
We have always been His friends,
But now He is the king!"

Thank You, Jesus, for being my king! I will be so happy to see You when You come! Amen.

Theme: God's Word

Jesus Comes Again, Part 2

When Jesus comes again, His friends will not be the only ones to see Him. The Bible tells us that Jesus will wake up the people who were mean to Him when He lived on earth, too. They will see that He really is God's Son and the King of the universe. All these people will admit that Jesus is the king.

[Sing to the tune of "The Farmer in the Dell."]

"Now Jesus is the king;
Now Jesus is the king!
Once He was a man they hurt,
But now He is the king!"

Dear Jesus, hurry and come back so we can be with You! Amen.

Theme: God's Word

#178

Fun With Jesus

When Jesus comes back as king, He will take all His friends to His home in heaven. It will be much more beautiful and more fun than the best places here on earth. He will show us all the things He has made for us, and the places He has fixed for us to live in His home. We will be able to spend time with Him, talking face-to-face, instead of praying like we have to do now when we talk to Him. He will talk to us too and we will have a wonderful time together.

[Sing to the tune of "She'll Be Comin' 'Round the Mountain."]

"We'll spend lots of time with Jesus
  When He comes.
We'll spend lots of time with Jesus
  When He comes.
We'll spend lots of time with Jesus;
We'll spend lots of time with Jesus;
We'll spend lots of time with Jesus
  When He comes.

"We'll have so much fun with Jesus
  When He comes . . . ," etc.

Dear Jesus, I can hardly wait to come to Your home in heaven. Amen.

Theme: God's Word

Our New Earth

Materials: *construction paper, nature stickers, glue*

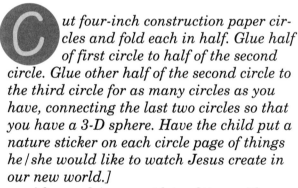

Cut four-inch construction paper circles and fold each in half. Glue half of first circle to half of the second circle. Glue other half of the second circle to the third circle for as many circles as you have, connecting the last two circles so that you have a 3-D sphere. Have the child put a nature sticker on each circle page of things he / she would like to watch Jesus create in our new world.]

After we have spent lots of time with Jesus in His home in heaven, He will bring us back to our earth. We'll be able to watch the most exciting thing that has ever happened. Jesus will create a new world out of this old one. He will burn up all the ugly places that are full of trash and pollution and dead things. He will make it a wonderful, perfect place just like He did for Adam and Eve.

We'll watch Jesus create flowers and animals, birds and trees. We'll be new, too, and never get sick or die. We'll live in our new earth home forever! Best of all, Jesus will move here to live with us.

Dear Jesus, I can hardly wait until we live together in the new earth! Amen.

Theme: God's Word

#180